Old-School Grit:
Lessons from History on Willpower, Tenacity, and Resilience

By Peter Hollins,
Author and Researcher at
petehollins.com

Table of Contents

CHAPTER 1: ERNEST SHACKLETON AND HIS CREW: AN INSPIRING STORY OF STRENGTH AND SURVIVAL — 7

CHAPTER 2: BEETHOVEN: NOT EVEN DEAFNESS WAS AN EXCUSE — 21

CHAPTER 3: THOMAS CARLYLE AND WRITING *THE FRENCH REVOLUTION* — 33

CHAPTER 4: THOMAS EDISON, THE LIGHTBULB, AND THE POWER OF TRYING 1000 TIMES — 47

CHAPTER 5: COLONEL SANDERS – A DELICIOUS STORY OF REJECTION — 59

CHAPTER 6: GALILEO AND THE BRAVERY TO STAND ALONE — 71

CHAPTER 7: THE BATTLE OF ZAMA: THE ROMAN'S SECRET TO WINNING — 83

CHAPTER 8: ALEXANDER THE GREAT AND THE LAND BRIDGE TO TYRE ISLAND — 97

CHAPTER 9: JULIUS CAESAR AND THE BATTLE OF ALESIA — 109

CHAPTER 10: THE BATTLE OF THERMOPYLAE 123

CHAPTER 11: SPARTACUS AND THE SERVILE WARS 137

SUMMARY GUIDE 150

Chapter 1: Ernest Shackleton and his crew: An inspiring story of strength and survival

Few stories of resilience are as amazing as that of the British Endurance Expedition, launched in 1914. The mission was to cross the Antarctic on foot, but sadly, this lofty goal was never to be achieved. Instead, the Endurance mission took a completely different shape: the ship, aptly named Endurance, got trapped in thick sheet ice on its journey out. The crew of Endurance was stranded for months in the ice as they battled abject cold, hunger, desperation, and even insanity.

The expedition leader, Ernest Shackleton, first led his men to abandon the trapped ship to the safety of nearby Elephant Island, and after that, he bravely left his crew to seek help. Because of his continued courage and discipline, he managed to save that crew, even though everything else was lost. The ship lay at the bottom of the ocean for 107 years before it was rediscovered recently in March 2022. As the ghost of this vessel was brought back to the surface, historians were again reminded of Ernest Shackleton and his crew.

But who was Shackleton, and what exactly happened on the expedition?

There were actually two ships – one called the Ross Sea Party on the ship Aurora that would drop supplies for the other, the Endurance. On this ship were 69 dogs, a tomcat, 27 men, and one ship stowaway, who was later put to work as a steward.

The expedition leader was Shackleton, who saw the voyage as a way to make a name for himself by establishing a base on the Weddell sea coast. Setting out in August, the ship was trapped in thick sheet ice in the Wendell Sea by December that year, and there was nothing the crew could do to free her. Though they could move the vessel for a little while, eventually the ice surrounded them so they could not budge either forward or backward. As the ice creaked and shifted, it took the ship with it, slowly drifting the men off course and crushing the hull bit by bit. They had been within only a day's reach of their destination, but with every day spent trapped, they drifted further away.

For ten long months, the crew sat on the trapped ship, waiting out the winter. One of the ship's doctors, Alexander Macklin, later wrote that Shackleton, "did not rage at all, or show outwardly the slightest sign of disappointment; he told us simply and calmly that we must winter in the Pack; explained its dangers and possibilities; never lost his optimism and prepared for winter."

For months, Shackleton tried to lead his men through the perilous Antarctic ice packs on dwindling provisions and scant morale. But he could not ignore the writing on the wall – they were going nowhere and running out of provisions. As seasoned sailors know, "What the ice gets, the ice keeps." Waiting patiently was a recipe for certain death.

Shackleton eventually ordered the crew to abandon ship, and in good time too, since it sank shortly afterwards – around 28 days later. The team escaped with their lives on just 3 lifeboats. They made difficult decisions about which of the barest essentials to take, discarding everything else. Most of the smaller dogs and the cat were shot, and the rest of their possessions were left behind to go down with the ship. It was gut-wrenching, but the ordeal was just getting started.

Try to imagine it: these 6 men braved the frozen wilderness in a small boat roughly 7m or 22 feet long and pressed on in this way for 800 miles, heading for the whaling stations they knew they'd find in South Georgia. It's hard for people to understand the suffering they would have endured: battered by gale force winds and near constant freezing rain, the men huddled in groups, riddled with seasickness, wondering which giant ice cap would capsize the boat in an instant and kill them all... Shackleton even wrote later in his memoirs that they once encountered a tidal wave so enormous that he originally mistook it for the sky. Later, in his book *South!*, Shackleton recounts, "Huge blocks of ice, weighing many tons, were lifted into the air and tossed aside as other masses rose beneath them. We were helpless intruders in a strange world, our lives dependent upon the play of grim elementary forces that made a mock of our puny efforts."

It's hard to imagine that these were men who had already gone through one unthinkable trial and had started this second journey cold, miserable, hungry, and ill. The crew had already lived for months trapped on board the Endurance in the ice floes. And now they were pitted against the merciless elements, each of them likely resigned to the fact that they would die. It was later reported that half the men on the boats were already mad, and some were viciously ill with dysentery. Some were chronically sleep-deprived, not having rested for 80 hours or so.

Finally, exhausted and barely holding things together, they reached the uninhabited Elephant Island. When they set foot on that dry land, it had been a staggering 497 days since the Endurance first set sail. Shackleton's second-in-command, Frank Wild, led the team to create a makeshift shelter out of two upturned lifeboats. The third boat was their last hope. Giving himself ten days to recover and prepare, Shackleton then left to seek help. He took with him five other men and set sail on the third lifeboat named "James Caird."

This time, they knew what to expect. They'd wake every morning to beat the ice out of the sails and bail freezing water from the boat before pushing on. The punishing winds howled and tossed the fragile boat on the open seas, and the men, with their last splinters of hope barely intact, somehow found it in them to keep rowing until they reached their destination.

After 17 further days of fighting to survive, they landed on the shores of South Georgia. The men rested briefly before the marathon hike of 36 hours across the island, finally finding Stromness Whaling station. It took beating out a path that no human had walked before, over mountain peaks and through icy terrain and frozen cliffs, but they did it – to the astonishment of those at the whaling station.

Can you imagine the sight of these three men turning up in the middle of nowhere? After nearly two years of suffering and desperation, they had long, stringy beards, ruined clothing, and gaunt faces. Thoralf Sørlle, the station manager, was so shocked at the sight of them that he turned and wept when Shackleton explained what had happened.

From there, Shackleton could arrange for a rescue ship to fetch the 22 sailors that still remained on Elephant Island. Again, this was a story of one disaster after another. The first ship that Shackleton launched ran out of fuel and was forced to turn back. A vessel offered by Uruguay made it to within 100 miles of Elephant Island before ice packs forced it to give up and return. It took several more attempts, but eventually the Chilean government agreed to lend him a small tugboat, called Yelcho. Heading back, Shackleton must have secretly feared the worst, wondering about the men he'd left behind. He had taken a full 128 days to return to them with help. As he approached, he noticed a smoke signal emerging from the makeshift shelter, and soon the men emerged, calling to him – all of them had made it.

In the meantime, Frank Wild had been tasked with keeping spirits up on the desolate Island wasteland. Every single morning, he would instruct the crew to prepare their belongings and get ready, since Shackleton might return any day now. Despite how despondent and despairing the crew felt, Wild kept it up. Many of the men had utterly given up and had resigned themselves to their fate, rather than keep clinging to hope. Their daily life was one of misery and privation, and they had little to do but ruminate on their doomed fate and boil up seal bones for nourishment. But that fateful morning on day 128, Shackleton really *did* return, and the crew was packed and ready, not quite believing that their nightmare was finally coming to an end. The crew all made it back to England, and years later, all were still alive and well.

Are you wondering what happened to the other ship, the Aurora? Sadly, this ship and its crew were essentially left to fend for themselves and were stranded. The commander of the ship and two other crew members perished, despite faithfully fulfilling their task of delivering food and supplies needed by the Endurance. The plan was to meet the Endurance in the Ross Sea, south of New Zealand, bringing supplies. So, although Shackleton's tale of endurance and daring rescue was the most compelling story to emerge from these events, the fact is that none of the original aims of the expedition were met – in fact, the Antarctic was only explored on foot decades later, in the 1950s by Sir Vivian Fuchs.

Whatever happened to Shackleton? Well, he never did reach the South Pole or cross the

Antarctic on foot, but he did attempt another expedition years later, with many of the same crew he had been with on the Endurance. They noted that he was never the same again. In fact, Shackleton died at just 47 years of age of a heart attack.

Granted, the days of high adventure and fantastic explorations to the poles seem like they belong to a bygone era, but the story of the Endurance and her crew still captures hearts and minds today. People continue to be astonished at just how much Shackleton and his men must have endured – how on earth could they have survived all that?

Take a look at any of the photographs of the crew throughout their doomed expedition and you cannot help but feel awe at the black and white faces peering back out at you. The ship was a small, wooden one with canvas sails, and the men aboard it were working with what we'd now consider rudimentary instruments. The men had, in total, spent *years* battling despair, insanity, starvation, exhaustion, and illness – all in a frighteningly hostile landscape where temperatures averaged roughly -66 F (-54 C).

Shackleton and his crew were forever considered impressive proof of the extent to which the human spirit can endure and prevail. Shackleton wrote a book about his experiences that gives a peek into his mind and allows us to guess at what it must have been like out there in the Antarctic wilderness:

> *"When I look back at those days I have no doubt that Providence guided us, not only across those snowfields, but across the storm-white sea that separated Elephant Island from our landing-place on South Georgia. I know that during that long and racking march of thirty-six hours over the unnamed mountains and glaciers of South Georgia it seemed to me often that we were four, not three. I said nothing to my companions on the point, but afterwards Worsley said to me, 'Boss, I had a curious feeling on the march that there was another person with us.' Crean confessed to the same idea. One feels 'the dearth of human words, the roughness of mortal speech' in trying to describe things intangible, but a record of our journeys would be incomplete without a reference to a subject very near to our hearts."*

Who was the fourth person on the journey with them? Shackleton knows that he can never fully express what he experienced out there, but we can conjecture. Perhaps he felt a divine spirit guiding and protecting him. Perhaps it was his own sense of hope and the fearsome refusal to give up and let go of his life. Perhaps it was simply raw human survival instinct, wordless and unconscious.

Many of the men did give up. Shackleton was a flawed man, who had certainly been criticized for his leadership skills over the course of his career, but one thing that people could agree on was that he took his duty to inspire hope and courage in his crew very seriously. Even though he was doubtless tormented internally, he never permitted himself to despair openly to the others.

Besides his clear faith in something greater than himself ("We had seen God in His splendors, heard the text that Nature renders. We had reached the naked soul of man" – *Shackleton's Incredible Voyage*), he also was a practical man. He speaks about the importance of grounding one's daily life in routine, about humility, and about simply getting on with what must be done, one way or another.

He remarked once, after his team had already endured countless months of sickness and starvation, the power of the little, everyday things:

> *"I heard one man say, "Cook, I like my tea strong." Another joined in, "Cook, I like mine weak." It was pleasant to know that their minds were untroubled, but I thought the time opportune to mention that the tea would be the same for all hands and that we would be fortunate if two months later we had any tea at all. It*

> *occurred to me at the time that the incident had psychological interest. Here were men, their home crushed, the camp pitched on the unstable floes, and their chance of reaching safety apparently remote, calmly attending to the details of existence and giving their attention to such trifles as the strength of a brew of tea."*

Brave hope and the will to survive are very grand endeavors – but they often play out in mundane ways. If we can focus on what is in front of us, no matter how small, we can find a kind of dignity in them. No matter how dire the situation is, we can take solace in ritual, in doing what little we can, and in sticking with routines – even if we don't quite have faith in them anymore.

Finally, perhaps the most noteworthy of Shackleton's attitudes was his seeming unwillingness to think about defeat even as a possibility. Like many deeply devoted and ambitious people, Shackleton simply did not allow himself to give up. "Difficulties," he claimed, "are just things to overcome." No matter the size of the difficulty, or how frequent they are, they were never a reason to stop, give up, or turn back. They were simply things that needed to be gone around – speed bumps rather than roadblocks that forever close off the path.

If we can replicate make this subtle shift in perspective, we allow ourselves to stay proactive and ask – how can I get around this?

If we assume that we will do everything we humanly can do to get around it, it simply becomes a matter of *how*. "Just when things looked their worst, they changed for the best. I have marveled often at the thin line that divides success from failure and the sudden turn that leads from apparently certain disaster to comparative safety." If you genuinely think this way about life, then no situation is so dire or so hopeless that it cannot one day turn completely and become something new. Hope, then, is like keeping your belongings packed and ready so that, when better things come, you are ready and waiting to seize them.

Real life example

Not many of us will ever endure the kind of suffering Shackleton and his men did, but we may well face other challenges, like major illness, poverty, or natural disasters. In more recent history, there are plenty of examples of people rising to extreme challenges, like the brave firefighters who worked tirelessly to retrieve survivors from the rubble of the bombing of the world Trade Center. They did precisely what Shackleton did; they dug deep and allowed the magnitude of their task to sober them and inspire them, then they refused to give up as they did what needed to be done. Shackleton's men were forced to find out what they were really made of. Senator John Kerry hints at the same phenomenon when he remarked of the 9/11 attacks, "It was the worst day we have ever seen, but it brought out the best in all of us."

Shackleton's lessons:

- Find purpose. Seek a deeper meaning and significance in your life, and, if it strengthens you, anchor yourself in religion or spirituality. Shackleton never felt alone during his most arduous challenges, and that's because he was a man of faith.
- When times are challenging, keep sane and even-keeled by engrossing yourself in the details of day to day life. Keep a routine, look after the basics of life, and if need be, find relieving distractions when things get especially difficult.
- Finally, don't give up. When you encounter a challenge, reframe the way you look at it: it's not the end. Difficulties are not a sign that your journey is over, just that the route has changed. Difficulties are just things to overcome. If you have hope, then you'll be prepared and ready to grasp opportunity when it does finally come your way.

Chapter 2: Beethoven: Not even deafness was an excuse

Most people know that the famous classical composer Ludwig van Beethoven was deaf, but have you ever stopped to consider what an incredible struggle this must have been? Perhaps we imagine that Beethoven was simply a genius; we see the end of his life centuries later, and the day-to-day details are lost to us.

Imagine for a second what it must be like to sit at a piano and play, but without being able to detect a single sound from it, in front of a large and expectant crowd. Imagine, too, you live in a time before hearing aids and where there is very little understanding of what it means to be deaf. Today, Beethoven is lauded as the brilliant musician he certainly was, but somewhat lost to history is the incredible resilience and strength it took to build that legacy.

Let's start at the beginning. Beethoven wasn't born deaf. He began to lose his hearing in his 20s, and by this time, he was fortunately already a respected musician and composer. Despite the gradual loss of his sense of hearing, he continued to perform – which in those days was expected of composers. In fact, Beethoven hid his disability for a time, with a degree of success, until it slowly became obvious what was happening. Composer Louis Spohr watched Beethoven perform in 1814 and sadly claimed the music was "unintelligible."

We cannot imagine how it must have felt for a man so accustomed to living in a world of sound to find himself slowly slipping into a realm of involuntary silence. By the time he was 45, Beethoven's hearing was completely gone, and there was no point in trying to perform publicly anymore. The composer, understandably, became more reclusive, and his friendship circle shrank to nothing. It wasn't just his music that suffered – he found communication with others increasingly difficult, until it was just easier to remain isolated.

Though he stopped performing, he was still a musician and always would be. It was in his blood. It was a way of life and all he knew how to do. So, he continued to compose. Using his knowledge of music theory, his memories, and his own unique brand of creativity, Beethoven composed music that he himself would never hear.

It's no surprise that his style changed drastically. What used to be light and playful became darker, heavier, and more contemplative. The piece of music called the "pastoral symphony" or the sixth symphony gives a fascinating peak into his mindset at this time. It is music that reflects the quietness of the countryside – a place where Beethoven had retreated in order to save his sanity. What Beethoven would prove to others is that music was a language and that, as long as he knew its syntax, he could create it, whether he had ears to hear it or not.

Today, Beethoven is held as one of the Western world's greatest classical composers – and many of his most loved and recognizable pieces came from the darkest, most difficult period of his life. Here was a man who showed that tragedy did not have to signal an end to creativity, to brilliance, or to strength. Even though Beethoven had to face each day knowing that another tiny little piece of his hearing would be lost, never to return, he continued to create. Even though he knew he would never again experience the joy of hearing his own masterpieces played live by an orchestra, he continued to create.

Let's not paint too rosy a picture: Beethoven was a complex character, and, in several letters written to his brother, historians find that he frequently expressed suicidal thoughts and deep despair at his own fate. Though Beethoven certainly had resilience and determination, he was also beset with feelings of embarrassment and self-pity. After being such a masterful and accomplished musician, the loss of his senses must have felt completely bewildering and disorienting. Can you imagine how cruel fate must have felt to him that it should have taken away the one sense that he most needed and cherished in life?

Often, when we think of much-admired historical heroes, we imagine that they are invulnerable. We see that they have endured much and triumphed, so we assume, wrongly, their journey was easy and that they never wavered along the way. Then, when faced with our own challenges and we feel scared, ashamed, angry or despondent, we can barely imagine that we have anything in common with these great figures from the past, who must have been magnificent masters of resilience.

But we do! This is because the most courageous and resilient among us don't possess any secret ability that we lack. They experience all the same emotions we do, and they struggle in the same ways. The only difference is that they also choose to *keep on going* despite it all. They are not brave because they are invulnerable; they are brave because they are just as vulnerable as the rest of us but choose not to let that stop them.

Beethoven had a unique method for "hearing" when his own ears failed him. He'd bite down on a stick that he then pressed against the wood of the piano so he could discern its vibrations as he played. Like Shackleton, it seems that it wasn't a question of "Should I continue to play the piano even though I am deaf?" but rather "*How* shall I play the piano, now that I am deaf?"

For Beethoven, then, resilience looks a lot like adaptability. His situation was unfortunate, and it hurt him considerably, but he also knew that he could always respond by making changes and adaptations and finding new solutions. Beethoven spent the rest of his life battling depression and trying to work around his disability, but work around it he did.

At the time, he must have felt like his deafness was a black spot on his career and something to be ashamed of. Isn't it ironic then, how many people love Beethoven today, not in spite of his disability, but because of it? What he teaches us, and perhaps what his disability taught him, is that adversity really is what you make of it. We admire and respect Beethoven as a musician *specifically because* we recognize deep down that his suffering makes him a better musician, not a worse one. We see that he was touched, deeply, by life and its mysteries. We see that adversity can be an invitation to growth, and we see that Beethoven rose to that challenge and created something from his predicament that elevated him above it all.

When his magnum opus, Symphony no. 9, was debuted, Beethoven stood beside the conductor, observing the orchestra and keeping time in his head. Despite not being able to hear it, the entire auditorium was there with him that day, wanting him to be a part of the beautiful creation that was unfolding – his gift to the world.

When the symphony was over, Beethoven couldn't hear the thunderous applause behind him. The conductor gently turned him so he could see. Granted, he never *heard* the cheers and cries of appreciation erupting from the enraptured crowd, but in that moment, he must have felt it in his very soul. He had gone beyond the mechanics of music – instead, something deeper and more profound had happened, and his music had reached beyond the ears and into the heart.

An article in 1932 *Time* magazine noted that, "He did not sense the applause which came afterwards until one of the soloists, a Fraulein Caroline Unger, turned him around so that his eyes could take it in. The music passed into the background then. The demonstration took a sudden, emotional turn as the people started shouting, beating their palms together still harder in an effort to assure the fierce-looking little man of their sympathy, their appreciation."

Today, this symphony (also called the "ode to joy") is instantly recognizable to people all over the world and has been enthusiastically embraced by people across history who heard something indescribable in its composition. Beethoven once said, *"Don't only practice your art, but force your way into its secrets, for it and knowledge can raise men to the divine."*

This was the boy who was taught to play the piano by his father, who would have him play hours daily even before his feet could properly reach the pedals. His father was an alcoholic, who frequently beat his son or deprived him of sleep. Beethoven was a talented musician, but he never felt like a genius – he struggled at school with math and reading, dropping out of school entirely by 10. When Beethoven was young, he managed to get the church organist to teach him to play the organ for free. By the age of 12, he was already studying with composer Gottlob Neefe and composing his own pieces.

Famously, he studied under Mozart for a time, who was much impressed with his abilities, and later would be a student of Haydn. Perhaps it was his father's early influence, but Beethoven embarked on a life characterized by non-stop learning. He was an eternal student of his craft, becoming almost obsessed with music.

As his career grew, he became known in Vienna for having a strong, determined personality. He was known as difficult to work with, careless of his appearance and often late! He once told a wealthy patron, Prince Lichnowsky, "Prince, what you are, you are through chance and birth; what I am, I am through my own labor. There are many princes and there will continue to be thousands more, but there is only one Beethoven."

Was this arrogance or just a rock-solid belief in his own abilities and his life's purpose? Well, many claimed that, when it came to what mattered – music – he was not in the least arrogant. When his opera *Fidelio* flopped, he took his critics complaints and addressed them diligently. This shows us that, while he might have appeared as a diva, it was only because he was acting in service of something greater.

It was this unwavering commitment to the purity of his craft that enabled Beethoven to be the first musician of his time to write and sell music directly to publishers rather than be commissioned by the royal court. Many have claimed that Beethoven was the first "music entrepreneur" and a real innovator of his time. He was, in short, a leader, and his own belief in himself and his purpose was the source of this strength and certainty.

Many people look back at the stories of the ultra-successful and wonder, "How did they find such success, despite all the adversity they faced?" In truth, the ultra-successful have found a way to succeed because of and with their adversity. Beethoven made a success of his life, not in spite of the unique and flawed human being he was, but precisely because of it. His deafness, his relentless focus on his craft, and the desire to elevate it to glorious heights, his idiosyncrasies, the loss of his hearing – all of it was a *part of* the unique gift he could offer the world.

What allowed Beethoven to do what he did? What allowed him to endure his hardship and become the prolific creator of works that are still adored today?

In the same way that Shackleton found immense strength and courage in his faith, Beethoven found that same well of conviction and determination in his own vision. While deaf, Beethoven created symphonies "in his head." But really, all innovators, creators, and dreamers create things this way. We must all hold something in our heads first, before we can bring it to life in the outside world. We will never know whether the music he created was an accurate reflection of the splendor and beauty Beethoven could imagine in his mind's eye, but we do know that he worked tirelessly to bring his vision to life.

It's this ability to hold onto the purity of your vision that can seemingly inspire people to keep going, no matter the challenges they face. Beethoven not only had a distinct sound, but the way he conducted his life was also his own. He was a musician whose life was guided by principle and excellence. We don't usually think of artistic integrity as a source of resilience, but think Beethoven pressed on because he knew he had something within him that *he needed to share*, and he would do whatever he could to get that music out there, one way or another.

Now, few of us are genius musicians like Beethoven was. We might not even consider ourselves talented in *any* area. Nevertheless, we all possess our own unique voice, our specific vision, and our distinctive will. Even in your darkest moments, know that you too can elevate yourself "to the divine" if you consistently try not to be just competent, merely excellent, but to push your craft to the very pinnacle of what it can be.

In the face of *that* as your mission, what could a few practical impediments do to stop you?

Beethoven's story teaches us that effort can be redemptive. Hard work can ennoble us. It can give us meaning and purpose, so that if we are beset by adversity and challenges, we are more than equipped to find our way through it. If you're not sure what "the divine" means here, all you have to do is listen to the final movements of the 9th symphony!

When we have an end goal in mind, off on the horizon, we fortify ourselves against any difficulty that plagues us in the present. We keep our eyes fixed on what could be. What else does a composer do but imagine all the beautiful things that *could exist* but don't yet? If you keep reminding yourself that you can be a conduit through which new and better things can emerge, then you may find you have the same energy and conviction as Beethoven, no matter what your unique challenges are.

Real life example

Most people have heard of Aimee Mullins because of the amazing TED talk she gave – still one of TED's most popular and inspiring. Born with a condition that required both of her legs to be amputated, Aimee never let her disability stop her. In fact, she competed against able-bodies athletes and in the Paralympics, going on to become a public speaker and even a model and actress. Aimee has some pretty astonishing words of wisdom: "The only true disability is a crushed spirit."

Beethoven's lessons:

- Dig deep and connect to your overarching life's purpose. What matters most to you? What do you care about

achieving here on earth more than anything else? Allow this conviction to give you strength to weather any obstacles on the way.
- Be true to yourself. Beethoven really did things his way. This wasn't always easy, but his commitment to his own authentic artistic vision gave him the courage to try things that others might not have wanted to risk. In difficult times, lean on your strengths – those unique insights and perspectives that nobody else could offer the world but you.
- Finally, be adaptable. When one path closes to you, look around for the paths that are still open. Refuse to dwell on what is missing, what is not working, or what is difficult. Instead, constantly turn your attention to what is possible, what resources you still have, and what opportunities are still there to be tapped.

Chapter 3: Thomas Carlyle and writing *The French Revolution*

It's never about how many times you fall, but how many times you get up.

The story of the Scottish historian and author Thomas Carlyle is one that will surely motivate and inspire all those people who've felt that they had to "start all over again at square one" in life. Have you ever spent time carefully crafting a text message only to backspace too aggressively and accidentally delete everything you've written? Well, this is broadly the story of Carlyle's life... multiplied by about a million.

To tell the story of Carlyle, though, we need to tell a few of the stories that formed the historical background in which he was working. During the years of the French Revolution and for some time afterwards, political, economic, and social upheaval was so intense people must have believed they were in the end times. The heads of noble men and women were chopped off, stuck onto pikes, and paraded around town by raucous mobs. There was a spirit of liberty, fraternity, and equality in the air but also mass public violence, chaos, and disorder in the streets and general mayhem the likes of which would shock even those of us who've lived through the last five years!

Let's introduce a few key characters: Maximilien de Robespierre was a lawyer and statesman and widely regarded as a key figure in the French Revolution, campaigning all his life for woman's suffrage, the abolition of slavery, and the principles of democracy. His role as a "public accuser" led to him agitating for the fall of the French monarchy and, ultimately, to 40,000 people being sentenced to death by guillotine. His days were limited, though, and eventually Robespierre would die by the sword, so to speak. In the chaos that ensued after he was beheaded, general Napoleon Bonaparte appeared on the scene, and gradually, order was restored.

The story that unfolded was one that inspired Charles Dickens to write *A Tale of Two Cities* – which is a novel that sheds light on the difficult, tragic, and sometimes horrific aspects of the revolution. But Dickens himself was inspired by another great author: Thomas Carlyle. After reading Carlyle's historic trilogy on this incredibly complex episode in history, Dickens was moved to create his own contribution.

Carlyle was born in 1795 and made his mark as a historian keenly interested in "great men" – i.e. those singular leaders around which significant historic events seem to organize. In his later treatise, *On Heroes and Hero Worship and the Heroic in History,* he outlined what would later be called the "Great Man Theory." He was a well-regarded Victorian satirist, essayist, and teacher and was renowned for a few controversial opinions in his time – he was notorious for a scathing and fearless style of political and social criticism, and he took his social role as a commentator and historian very seriously.

The way Carlyle wrote about history had a dramatic effect on the way historians spoke about and documented the past. The impact of this shift is difficult to comprehend for those of us living in an ideological world he arguably helped to create. His study of leadership and the theory it produced arose from Carlyle's interest in Napoleon's stabilization of a revolution-ravaged France. Carlyle was interested in how often great men were, in fact, quite complex individuals, and he was concerned with the way that this complex history was written. He would frequently argue that historical figures should not be judged on trivial mistakes but rather their larger, genuine displays of heroism. The fact that notable figures had small flaws or the occasional unfashionable opinion should not, he felt, distract from their overarching achievements. It's likely his passion for this project stemmed from his own colorful history as a person unafraid of digging for "the real story."

Despite calling economics a "dismal science," Carlyle had a close friend and economist, John Stuart Mill, who believed enormously in Carlyle's talents and urged him to consider writing about the French Revolution, with his help. Carlyle agreed and labored for four months over a manuscript that would tell the story of the French Revolution, paying respectful and careful attention to nuance, paradox, and complexity, not to mention the complicated figures involved, such as Napoleon. And here's where our main story begins.

Carlyle worked by hand because, in 1835, typewriters were an uncommon luxury for the super-rich, and even paper and ink were precious. He sent the first draft of the first volume of the book to Mill to review. From there, Mill took the manuscript to a friend's home... and promptly forgot it there. The servant cleaning that room, unaware of what the manuscript was, crumpled it up and used it to light the fire. Oops.

The next day, an understandably sheepish Mill turned up at Carlyle's house with a pile of heavily charred pages packed into a satchel. He could say nothing as he presented the tragedy to his friend, filled with pity and regret. Could you imagine what it was like to see the fruits of four months' labor literally reduced to smithereens?

Perhaps Carlyle, who had made the study of leadership his life's work, had learnt something about dignity and composure during adversity. He instantly forgave Mill and refused his offer of payment and apology. In fact, he later wrote how he endeavored to hide from his friend his disappointment, to spare him from feeling worse.

But he was disappointed – devastated, even. Carlyle was broke. He hadn't made any money from writing for over a year at that point and was burning through his savings. He had battled depression and many other personal demons for years. He *needed* that manuscript. He had worked hard, and it had all come to precisely nothing. He had done the thing he knew in his heart would bring honor and meaning to his life: identify a goal and work with everything in him until that goal was achieved. He had done that, and admirably. Yet he was faced with a crushing realization: all of that was gone now. He was back at square one.

That night, Carlyle had a dream where his deceased father and brother came to him and urged him not to give up his work, even though all appeared lost. In the morning, he contacted

Mill to tell him he'd accept the money after all – so that he could buy enough paper to start over again.

He began to write the second and third volumes and then, when he was ready, tried to reconstruct the first volume from what he could remember. Remarkably, Carlyle ended up completing the manuscript by its original deadline, and all three volumes of *History of the French Revolution* were published in 1847. Not only that, but the work was then, as it is now, lauded as a best-selling classic of history. Today, more than 200 years later, the work is still cherished and read by those who continue to appreciate its comprehensive and nuanced analysis.

If Carlyle had not found the courage that day to dust himself off and start over again, the book would never have been published and Dickens would never have been inspired to write A Tale of Two Cities. And who knows what other works were then inspired by Dickens and so on? When Carlyle was urged in a dream not to abandon his mission, perhaps he wasn't aware of the repercussions of his choice to carry on – or, perhaps, it was precisely *because* he knew how important a story it was that he found energy to carry on.

Like so many of the great leaders that fascinated Carlyle, he was a complex and melancholic individual, who threw himself into his work, often choosing subjects that had a flavor of "divine drama" about them. In fact, Carlyle came to see history as "divine scripture" and his narrative of the unfolding of the French Revolution has now become the dominant one. If you believe that the French Revolution was an epic tale of retribution and punishment meted out on the foolish and greedy nobility of the day, then you have already partaken of Carlyle's massively influential perspective, perhaps without even knowing it.

Carlyle turned against his religious upbringing, but his work was forever colored by his own sense of the epic universal battle between good and evil, the drama of order versus chaos, overseen by powerful, larger-than-life heroes and villains – such as General Lafayette and Robespierre. Unlike many of the historians of his time, Carlyle wrote passionately and with fearsome moral conviction. Take a look at one paragraph from the book in question:

> *"But figure his thought, when Death is now clutching at his own heart-strings, unlooked for, inexorable! Yes, poor Louis, Death has found thee. No palace walls or life-guards, gorgeous tapestries or gilt buckram of stiffest ceremonial could keep him out; but he is here, here at thy very life-breath, and will extinguish it. Thou, whose whole existence hitherto was a*

chimera and scenic show, at length becomest a reality: sumptuous Versailles bursts asunder, like a dream, into void Immensity; Time is done, and all the scaffolding of Time falls wrecked with hideous clangour round thy soul: the pale Kingdoms yawn open; there must thou enter, naked, all unking'd, and await what is appointed thee! Unhappy man, there as thou turnest, in dull agony, on thy bed of weariness, what a thought is thine! Purgatory and Hell-fire, now all-too possible, in the prospect; in the retrospect,--alas, what thing didst thou do that were not better undone; what mortal didst thou generously help; what sorrow hadst thou mercy on? Do the 'five hundred thousand' ghosts, who sank shamefully on so many battle-fields from Rossbach to Quebec, that thy Harlot might take revenge for an epigram,--crowd round thee in this hour? Thy foul Harem; the curses of mothers, the tears and infamy of daughters? Miserable man! thou 'hast done evil as thou couldst:' thy whole existence seems one hideous abortion and mistake of Nature; the use and meaning of thee not yet known. Wert thou a fabulous Griffin, devouring the works of men; daily dragging virgins to thy cave;--clad also in scales that no spear would pierce: no spear but Death's? A Griffin not fabulous

> *but real! Frightful, O Louis, seem these moments for thee.--We will pry no further into the horrors of a sinner's death-bed."*

Carlyle saw what unfolded in France as a divine judgment against the selfishness of the upper classes, and he saw his role as a faithful documentarian and story-teller of these classical epics. Let's be honest for a moment: most of us can hardly imagine the life of Thomas Carlyle or make much sense of his vision of history, now confined to history himself. But if we dwell for a moment on his story, we can appreciate that his life was one of conviction, achievement, and hard work – not to mention resilience.

What can we learn from a man like Carlyle? If we could travel back in time and ask him directly, what advice would he give those people wishing to live a life of meaning, purpose, and value?

Carlyle once said, "What we become depends on what we read after all of the professors have finished with us. The greatest university of all is a collection of books." The man adored books and was widely read. In fact, he believed that "All that mankind has done, thought, gained, or been; it is lying as in magic preservation in the pages of books."

It was no secret that Carlyle held the virtues of reading, self-learning, and authorship in the highest esteem. For him, the only thing more epic than being a man of great historical significance was learning, reading, and writing about such men.

The story about Carlyle starting his life's work all over again after his first attempt was burnt to ash is a nice, neat anecdote. But if we dig deeper, we can see *why* he felt so driven to keep on writing, no matter what. Though a little big-headed, Carlyle took his duty as a record keeper of the divine saga of his time very, very seriously. He didn't merely continue his manuscript because he felt like it – he did so because of the unwavering conviction that he had been visited by his deceased family from beyond the grave, exhorting him to push on.

Now, whether you agree with Carlyle's take on history, whether you like his style, or whether you consider the loss of four months' work a life-altering tragedy is irrelevant. What Carlyle teaches us – along with many other great leaders and heroes in history – is what "greatness" is. Have you ever thought about it, really? What sets apart these larger-than-life personages that seem to be etched in the human record?

Carlyle gives us a hint: it's a sense of one's own grandness, the power of sincerity and self-belief, and the willingness to bring a little of the otherworldly into one's own life. Carlyle loved drama, and he took his life and his work seriously. *This* is where his resilience came from. Like Ernest Shackleton, he was able to do what he did because he had a vision of his life as somehow bigger and grander than the barest, most immediate details of his existence. Carlyle once claimed his life's ambition was to die of exhaustion rather than boredom. He resented mediocrity, cowardice, and slovenliness. Being a hero, then, is about playing large!

Finally, something that makes Carlyle stand out as a historical figure is his keen intuition about the power of narrative. He understood the magic hidden in words and knew that style, intention, and context made meaning. He knew that the hero's journey was one that was best documented in mankind's earliest incarnation of history: the epic tale. From him, we can learn that much strength and resilience are possible if you only know the right perspective to take!

If you are a hero on a divine mission, then losing your life's work in one day is not the end of the road – it's merely one episode in the grand story, one battle in the war. In fact, you could write it so that your adversity is a profound teacher, your trouble an opportunity to cultivate greatness, and your adversities your greatest friends, since they teach you all the ways you are actually better than you previously allowed yourself to believe.

Real world example

In 1984, an enormous fire broke out at Pinewood Studios, burning down the biggest film set in the world at the time. The $30 million 20th Century Fox mega-fantasy film "Legend" was being filmed, and the damage was extreme, with two stagehands sustaining second-degree burns. The fire erupted during a lunch break and, when it encountered some gas cylinders, was soon out of control. The crew was only 10 days away from wrapping up the film.

The art department completely lost a complicated and expensive forest scene that had taken hundreds of man hours to build. Though a gargantuan tragedy by anyone's standards, director Ridley Scott quickly set to work adapting the schedule, moving people to a new set, and making sure workers doubled down to rebuild the set. It was a bitter, bitter loss, but as they say, the show must go on. And it did.

Carlyle's Lessons:

- Live large. Take your mission seriously and choose to be a hero in your own epic saga of triumph and overcoming.
- Endless resilience is possible when you tap into your deepest convictions and beliefs. Find that thing you are most passionate and resolute about and allow

it to animate all your efforts. That way, any obstacle is perceived as a minor inconvenience, just a trifle on the bigger, more important path you're on.
- Read. Educate yourself and absorb knowledge wherever you can. Carlyle built a complex and sophisticated worldview because he was able to read widely, and this view would forever act as a buffer against adversity and a source of strength during dark times.

Chapter 4: Thomas Edison, the lightbulb, and the power of trying 1000 times

From the mists of antiquity to a more recent and probably more familiar story, we now explore the great Thomas Edison, who can certainly teach us about resilience, discipline, and finishing what you start. Most of us are at least somewhat acquainted with the story of Edison and his unfathomable determination – i.e., "I haven't failed, I have just found 10,000 ways that don't work."

It may not seem like it at first, but Edison shares quite a few characteristics with the other people on our list. Like Ernest Shackleton, he was not a man to cave in and give up; like Beethoven, he was flexible and committed to doing the work he knew in his heart was most valuable; and like Thomas Carlyle, he was not afraid of starting again.

The anecdote is that Edison tried 1000 times before he finally figured out his most famous invention, the lightbulb. Actually, the truth is more impressive – he tried *2774 times*! To be truthful, Edison did not actually invent the lightbulb but rather refined it and enabled its widespread commercial success. It was Humphrey Davy who first invented the electric arc lamp and Warren de la Rue who proposed the now recognizable design of a coiled filament inside a vacuum tube. Joseph Swan made the next upgrade by replacing expensive platinum filaments with carbonized paper ones, and later cotton.

The Canadian Woodward and Evan's light was filed to be protected by patent in 1874, but in 1879, Edison bought out these patents and, along with a few tussles with other patent holders, eventually took over and became the household name associated with lightbulbs. But Edison was an uncommon blend of businessman *and* scientist, and he certainly made a significant contribution to the lightbulb as we know it today.

He got to work developing a filament that was formed from carbonized bamboo. This version could burn for 1200 hours and be mass produced, two factors that allowed Edison's version to dominate the market. Let's return to the near-mythical story of the "1000 failures" though. It's hard to quantify exactly what counts as one failure, but Edison kept meticulous records, and 2774 is the number of experiments it took to reach the point of commercial success.

As it turns out, the famous Edison quote is not quite true to life, and Edison is reported to have said something similar in relation to his work with the battery, not the lightbulb. In the 1920 biography *His Life and Inventions* by Frank Dyer and T.C. Martin, Walter S. Mallory (a friend of Edison) is said to have told the following story:

> *This [the research] had been going on more than five months, seven days a week, when I was called down to the laboratory to see him [Edison]. I found him at a bench about three feet wide and twelve feet long, on which there were hundreds of little test cells that had been made up by his corps of chemists and experimenters. I then learned that he had thus made over nine thousand experiments in trying to devise this new type of storage battery, but had not produced a single thing that promised to solve the question. In view of this immense amount of thought and labor, my sympathy got the better of my judgment, and I said: 'Isn't it a shame that with the tremendous amount of work you have done you haven't been able to get any results?' Edison turned on me like a flash, and with a smile replied: 'Results! Why,*

> *man, I have gotten lots of results! I know several thousand things that won't work!'*

So, whether it was 1000 or 10,000 attempts, or whether it was for one design or another, the point remains: even accomplished inventors do not achieve "results" on the first few tries. And while Edison's attitude is viewed today with admiration and respect, it is in fact nothing more than the natural perspective of a scientist.

In science, the goal is not lofty or ego-based – you simply wish to know, to uncover, to discover, to illuminate your own understanding. Then, you employ the meta-tool called the scientific method, which allows you to proceed in a series of strategic steps on your path towards knowledge. You form hypotheses, you design experiments to test it, you observe and analyze your results, come to conclusions, then try again.

On this path, there is no success or failure, per se. If you set out to see if a hypothesis is true, and you discover that it is not, then you haven't "failed" to prove it – you have simply discovered its untruth. The accomplishment, if it can be called that, is not smaller than if you *had* discovered your hypothesis was true. Thus, trial and error is not adversity, obstacle, or difficulty. It is simply the path – the *only* path – that we take to arrive at knowledge.

Edison is also quoted as saying in a 1903 Harper's magazine issue that, "Genius is one percent inspiration, ninety-nine percent perspiration." Even though Edison was widely hailed as an inspiring genius (he still is!), he didn't see himself this way. Rather, he understood that achievements are gained one step at a time – and many of those steps will be "failures." Being smart is nice, but it's actually consistent, dedicated hard work that gets things done.

Edison was one of the world's most prolific inventors, but it's easy to forget just how much he invented that *wasn't* all that great! Today we all associate him with the lightbulb, but Edison had almost 2000 patents to his name – such as for the phonograph and the motion picture camera – and many of them have been forgotten or subsequently improved upon by other scientists. But *all* of his work was important. Every experiment, every guess, every fresh attempt or flop or accident or unexpected surprise – all of it was a part of what allowed Edison to create the legacy he is known for today.

Certain people are capable of extraordinary resilience, achievement, and discipline, not because they never encountered difficulties, but because of the *way they framed* those difficulties. Long before life coaches and self-help gurus were talking about the power of mindset, these leaders, inventors, and strategists were showing that success really does start in the mind.

Today, psychologist Carol Dweck's model of a "growth mindset" gives us a framework to understand these ultra-successful people and the perspectives that informed their greatness. For Dweck, everyone in life will experience setbacks, hardships, disappointments, losses or failures. No question. However, there are two very different ways to respond to them, and they each come down to the person's conception of themselves.

With a growth mindset, you see yourself as capable of growth and change, which means that you understand that achievement is a process. Accordingly, you embrace challenge and difficulty because you know it's the very thing that allows you to learn and improve. You put in the effort and you keep going despite difficulties – because difficulties are merely seen as temporary.

With a fixed mindset, however, you see your characteristics (discipline, intelligence, strength) as fixed – either you're born with them or you're not. This means that effort doesn't change anything, and you might as well do what you can to *avoid* challenge, since it's not possible to learn from it. You'll give up at the first impediment and quietly resent others for their success, instead of being inspired by it.

If your perspective is built on growth, then you're able to think, "I don't know how to do this yet, but I'll figure it out." From a fixed mindset, you simply conclude. "I don't know how to do this. It can't be done... ever." Can you see how all the people we've covered so far have demonstrated, in their own way, a powerful growth mindset?

Again, it's almost as though the word "resilience" is not quite right. It implies that we are out there in the world, facing the onslaught of attacks, setbacks, painful losses and so on, continually raining down on us. "Resilience" is then how good we are at tolerating it all without complaining! But the people who are *really* resilient don't actually hold this view. They don't see setbacks, failures, or disappointments in the same way. If something doesn't work, they don't frame it as a tragedy. They just note that it doesn't work. This immediately frees them up to do something important: figure out what *does* work.

Rather than seeing things that don't go their way as some uncomfortable hardship dished up by the universe, they remain curious and open-minded, like scientists. What does their result – any result – teach them? Failure, you see, is as important to your learning as success. If you're a scientist, your success is only defined by your understanding. So long as you try, you have data, and that data is valuable.

With a growth mindset, you are in continual dialogue with reality, rather than passively accepting whatever you can see on first look. You ask questions, and you keep asking them. If your questions go nowhere, you ask new ones: "What are the right questions to ask here? What am I missing?" If you are not getting the results you want, you investigate the kind of tool you need to do so – sometimes, that tool is yourself. You need to ask, *what kind of a person do I need to be to achieve my goal?*

There are many great lessons we can learn from someone like Thomas Edison, but most of them spring from this fundamental perspective on life. Edison teaches us a subtle mindset shift: we should not strive to avoid failing, but to *fail better*. Can we embrace our failures and learn from them? Can we make our failures mean something?

Consider that there were many inventors and scientists working on electric light and various bulb designs in Edison's lifetime. Many of them might have been more intelligent or luckier than Edison. But none of this would have mattered if they had made a few attempts and then given up shortly after. Today, we consider Edison a great inventor, but most of us would harshly judge someone who tried something 1000 times and still hadn't figured out how to do it, right? That's the difference. Edison was willing to continue trying long after other scientists and innovators would have given up in frustration. In fact, by sheer volume, Edison failed more times than many other competent inventors had even tried.

This is its own kind of resilience. It's not born from a sense of divine right and conviction (like Carlyle), and it doesn't stem from a sincere passion about your life's ultimate purpose (like Beethoven). Instead, it is something infinitely practical. It didn't work? Try again. That's all. Edison was reported to work sometimes 18 hours a day. He said, "Our greatest weakness lies in giving up. The most certain way to succeed is always to try just one more time."

The next time you face an outcome that you don't like or didn't expect, don't fight with it or assume that it's all over for you – this is just more of the "fixed mindset" talking. Instead, get curious. Learn more. You will instantly find that all the things you were calling "problems" actually aren't – it's just life, and you are simply trying to find your way through it. Your attitude and response to failure matter more than the failure itself.

Naturally, you don't have to be a literal scientist to cultivate this kind of mindset. And invention, hard work, and originality are not confined to any single area of life. If you think that you're not the kind of person who belongs in the same class as Edison, think again – he was a man who struggled with his early schooling and experienced poverty growing up.

According to him, "If we did all the things we are capable of, we would literally astound ourselves." Are you one of those people that walks around, convinced that their limitations and flaws will always hold them back, that things are bad and won't get better? Well, look around at the world. How much of it was created by people who refused to believe that was true? Fear and self-doubt can be crippling, but if we are courageous and adventurous, who knows what we could achieve?

Almost everyone (scratch that, *everyone*) will occasionally reach a point in life where they feel they are at a dead end. It may not look like there are many options available to them, and they're all but ready to throw in the towel. But think of this way: there is always something better out there… you just haven't found it yet. The perfect lightbulb design was always there, waiting for the man who was patient and dedicated enough to travel the distance required to reach it. Whatever is bothering you right now, change your perspective by realizing that a potential solution is out there – you're just not there yet.

One way to look at resilience is to see it as an ability to endure misfortune. But the best way to endure is paradoxically not to endure at all – get up and do something about it! If you don't like something, change it. If your whole plan has blown up in your face, dust yourself off and make another, better plan to replace it.

It's only human to feel overwhelmed at times or to get discouraged by endless setbacks and problems. But try to remember that there are also endless possibilities. If you think you've tried everything – well, you haven't! Look again. Realize that dwelling on problems doesn't make them go away, but taking action brings you one step closer to something better.

Real life example

Have you ever heard of Traf-O-data? Probably not. But you have heard of the man who created it – Bill Gates. Traf-O-Data was just one of Gates's many flops and failures on his path to where he is now. Likewise, the "Apple Lisa" was a necessary failure along Steve Jobs' path to success, and Walt Disney's idea for Mickey Mouse was originally rejected by MGM because the studio felt that women would be afraid of mice. Failure is normal! These people had two main things in common: they all failed before they succeeded, and they all worked really, really hard to get to that success.

Thomas Edison's lessons:

- Change the way you think about failure. Challenge and adversity are the best teachers you will ever have in life. Instead

of getting upset when things don't go your way, become curious about what happened and why, then try again, but this time do it better!
- Forget about things like genius or innate talent. They're nice to have, but the people who get ahead are simply those who are willing to work hard and do it consistently.
- Adopt a growth mindset and constantly turn your attention, not to what is going wrong, but to the infinite world of the possible. There **is** a way out of your current predicament – how are you going to get from here to there?

Chapter 5: Colonel Sanders – A delicious story of rejection

Granted, you might not associate Kentucky Fried Chicken with discipline, dedication, and endurance, but these are exactly the qualities that allowed KFC's founding father, Colonel Harland David Sanders, to create the fried chicken empire we all know and love. In many ways, Sanders was the "Edison of fast food" and one of the century's first prominent entrepreneurs. He was born in 1890 and died in 1980, and the phenomenal social, cultural, and economic changes associated with that long period were in no small part his own doing.

First, let's clarify a few biographical details. The title of "colonel" is a real honorific, but one peculiar to the Commonwealth of Kentucky. It is not a military rank but something awarded to civilians who have achieved noteworthy accomplishments or else contributed to society in a remarkable or outstanding way. So, interestingly, there are many "Kentucky colonels," and each of them is recognized for their role as a kind of goodwill ambassador for the state of Kentucky, sharing its culture and traditions. That said, the title has gone to people from all walks of life, from celebrities, artists, businesspeople, politicians, and even royalty who have no particular connection to Kentucky.

Sanders didn't hit on his big idea from the start. Instead, he worked all kinds of jobs and was, at various points, an insurance salesman, farmer, lawyer, gas station operator, and steam engine stoker. He sold his first chicken at a diner in North Corbin, Kentucky during the Great Depression. The "secret recipe" combined with his technique of cooking chicken in a pressure fryer created the classic fried chicken now familiar to so many.

His first restaurant eventually closed, but he was beginning to wonder about the possibility of franchising his brand and scaling up. In 1952, the first officially named KFC restaurant was opened in South Salt Lake in Utah, and, just 12 years later, his success in the U.S was so phenomenal that he was able to sell the company to investors for what would today be around $17 million. Sanders was by then 73 years old, but in no way ready to quit, and became a kind of brand ambassador for the company. Sadly, towards the end of his life,

Sanders was reported to be unhappy with the standard of food that had now come to be served at restaurants all over the world and claimed that cost-cutting had reduced the food's quality.

Sanders died of leukemia at the age of 90. At that point, there were approximately 6,000 KFC branches in 48 countries all over the world, bringing in a combined $6.3 billion sales annually every year. Today, the number of restaurants is a whopping 25,000 in 145 countries – which is more countries than McDonald's!

So much for the official KFC story, but what about Sanders as a person? Who was he, and can we learn anything from him when it comes to resilience?

It was in 1950 that Sanders was commissioned as a Kentucky colonel by then Governor Lawrence Wetherby. This was quite a turning point for him. In no time, he began living out the stereotypical vision of a colonel. The image you see of Sanders on the KFC branding? That wasn't how he always looked. In fact, he had to work at it, and at first people were not even sure if he was kidding or not. He grew a goatee, wore the quintessential white suit and black string tie, and embraced his new title.

Once this public image took root, Sanders never abandoned it for the rest of his days. For the final decades of his life as KFC brand ambassador, it was all he wore. His hair went white, and he bleached his mustache to match.

John Y. Brown Jr. claimed that he was "a brilliant man with a gourmet flair for food, a visionary and a great motivator, with the style of a showman and the discipline of a Vince Lombardi (a famous football coach)."

So, we know that he was slightly eccentric, and that people around him tended to admire his perseverance, dedication, and ambition. You don't build a massive restaurant empire from scratch without a few skills, no doubt! But what was the colonel's "secret recipe," so to speak?

Well, let's look at the timeline: Sanders was already in his sixties when he ran his initial restaurant. After it closed, he was flat broke. He actually retired and took his first social security check for the princely sum of $105. For many others, this would have been the end of the line. Old and getting older, there are not many pensioners who would choose this moment start a massive business venture, especially not one based on something as simple as fried chicken. He'd already had many failed jobs by then and three kids from a failed marriage under his belt.

But Sanders loved fried chicken. And he was really, *really* convinced that the world needed to taste his version. At first, he went around from restaurant to restaurant and tried a sales tactic that might have made most salesmen balk in horror. He offered to cook up a batch of his chicken there and then for the owners. If they agreed it was good, he'd arrange to have them sell his chicken at their restaurant.

And the rest was history, right? Nope. In a story that is more Edison-like than Edison's own story, Sanders was ultimately turned down 1009 times. Just picture that. More than 1000 times, someone shrugged and said, "Nah," to his big idea, and more than 1000 times, he carried on and kept going anyway. If he did this once a day every single day, it would have taken him almost 3 years. Imagine three solid years of daily rejection, and you have a peek inside the mind of Colonel Sanders. Is there anything *you're* so sure about that you would push through more than 1000 rejections to see it come to life?

If we're frank, most of us today have a vision of success that skews, shall we say, to the youthful. We love poring over "billionaire by 30" lists, get a thrill out of imagining that Mozart had composed his first symphony at 9 years old, and that Alexander the Great had built the largest empire in the known world before his thirtieth birthday (more on him later)!

If you happen to be in your thirties, forties, or older, there's absolutely no reason to think that your chance for success has passed you by. In fact, there are plenty of examples of brilliant people who only got started later in life. Julia Child published her first mega-seller cookbook at age 50, Toni Morrison won a Nobel Prize for literature when she was 62, and actor Steve Carrell didn't make an acting name for himself until he was 42.

Basically, if you're still alive, there's time!

Think about it: is there really any reason why, at some magically pre-determined age, you should suddenly be unable to act towards your dreams? What exactly happens at 30, 40 or 50 that means success is no longer on the cards for you? Sanders took just 12 years to build up a business he eventually sold for millions. He started late, but he believed in what he wanted to do, and that belief carried him through.

If we dig deeper into this, we may guess at other traits that helped the Colonel become *the* Colonel. When he found his stereotypical, white-suited image, he stuck with it. He lived the KFC brand day in and day out. But he wasn't always the Colonel – he had spent years in an assortment of roles and, by his own admission, failed at all of them.

We can imagine now that his perfect role as the colonel was somehow inevitable and just waiting for him in the future, but Sanders had to do something important to get there: he had to refuse to let the past define him. Too often, we let adversity, failure, and challenge in the past determine how much we are allowed to succeed in the future. Sanders could have defined himself as a failed lawyer, a down-and-out divorcee, or a retired gas station boy. He didn't.

This is an important point. When Sanders was visiting restaurants trying to convince people of the greatness of his special recipe, he didn't allow the hundreds of rejections to let him stop expecting a yes. No matter how many times you've failed, you can still succeed on your very next time. And once you do, all those failures won't matter.

Success is never guaranteed, but there is one guaranteed way to fail – give up!

You are only a failure if you give up and tell yourself that it's over. Persistence is not some superhuman feat, though. It's more like stubbornness! You don't always need to see the light at the end of tunnel. You don't have to pretend it isn't hard or scary. You don't even have to be sure that something will come through in the end. All you have to do is keep going. That's it.

Resilience is the kind of strength that often takes time to build. Rather than imagining that each passing day is somehow a failure, see it as one more steppingstone, one more opportunity to build on who you are, learn something, and cultivate the right mindset.

There are many advantages to starting late. For one, you are older and wiser (yes, wiser, even if you don't really feel like it!). You have experience. Younger people may have energy and enthusiasm, but how often does this fizzle out or take them in the wrong direction? We tend to think of passion as belonging to the young, but there is a kind of dogged determinism that belongs only to those who are old enough to understand what's really at stake. The fact that your time may be limited may be precisely the thing that allows you to weather current adversities and get serious about what you *really* want to do with your life. And, paradoxically, it's what allows you to take risks. What have you got to lose, really?

If you are currently facing adversity and feeling like a failure, take heart: you probably have only encountered a small fraction of the failure that Colonel Sanders endured. Think about that: if he had quit at the point that most people tend to quit, even he would not have found the success he did.

Finishing what you start is a kind of old-fashioned virtue that most of us don't appreciate much anymore. But often, your sense of failing in life or having undue hardship is really just a matter of having unrealistic expectations – were you secretly expecting that success would be much, much easier?

Some of the people we've covered in the book so far have had impressive lives. But to be fair, we only see the impressive parts. There were times when Carlyle was confused, grumpy, or under the weather. There were times when Beethoven must have been bored or irritated with music. There must have been times when Edison caught a cold or had a fight with a family member that made it hard for him to concentrate that day.

What Sanders can teach us is that, no matter what our goal is, there will be some unglamorous, boring, and unpleasant parts along the way. In fact, this is what the journey to greatness *is*: mostly not great! The people covered in these chapters are now well-known and respected, but there was a time when they had to act without that recognition. They worked hard *before* they were successful. So why should we expect to have a path any different? They would have had to put in hours, days, weeks, months, and years of consistent effort without anyone else believing in them and, in some cases, with the world actively pushing against them.

Resilience, then, is not just the ability to endure a momentary humiliation or setback. It's the strength to know that you will work hard and do what's required *consistently*, until the goal is achieved. We can imagine someone travelling back in time and telling all of the world's greatest entrepreneurs that, one day, they would be rich and successful beyond their wildest dreams.

Imagine someone going back in time and telling Bill Gates, Steve Jobs, or Warren Buffett, "Hey, keep going! You're on the right path!"

Wouldn't it be nice to have that for yourself? The truth is that resilient people *do* actually have it – they have a voice inside them, a conviction that they will get to where they're going, one way or another. They have faith in themselves and their plans. They have a vision, calling to them from the future. Maybe nobody else sees it yet, but they can. And so, while others are thinking, "Should I even bother? Why carry on with this path if it's so difficult right now and I'm not even guaranteed a good outcome?" the resilient people are thinking the opposite.

And *because* they think that way, they create a self-fulfilling prophesy. They work hard because they have convinced themselves it will amount to something. When facing an obstacle, they can still angle their necks and peek around the obstacle, keeping their eyes on what really matters, up ahead in the distance. In this way, they're resilient. They stick with their commitments.

Colonel Sanders wasn't necessarily smarter or more talented than others (we can see from his old jobs that he wasn't!). In fact, he might not have even had an especially good chicken recipe (a heretical statement, maybe). But what he did have was this special kind of conviction that never gave him permission to give up, no matter how many rejections or failures he experienced.

Real world example

Let's be honest for a moment – achieving wealth and fame is *not* the only way to make a success of your life. There's no need to make that your yardstick. But chances are you've come to a place in your own life (maybe a milestone birthday?) where you stop and ask what it all amounts to. Getting older gives us a unique opportunity to get real about our priorities, our resources, and how much we're willing to work for what we want.

There are older people who have figured this out – and those who haven't. There are likely people in your world right now that have some powerful lessons about resilience to teach, if you are willing to hear them. And these stories don't have to be epic to have meaning. It may be the uncle that pieced his life back together after losing his wife, the stay-at-home mom who launched an entirely new career at 50 after her children left for university, or the workaholic who realized after a triple bypass that he needed to rethink his lifestyle completely. Talk to the people – their insights may astound you.

Colonel Sanders lessons:

- It's never too late to start over, no matter how old you are. Colonel Sanders started

over in his sixties and still managed to create a business empire that would overtake those he might have considered younger and more talented than him. The past doesn't define who you are now, and it doesn't define who you can be in the future.
- Success takes time, and it takes consistent, diligent effort – there are no shortcuts for anyone. You don't have to be superhuman to be resilient and disciplined. All you need to do is refuse to give up. Don't pay attention to the flashy success stories you read about in the media – true accomplishment doesn't happen overnight, so be patient.
- If you're facing a setback, loss, or disappointment, consider adjusting your expectations. Sometimes being mentally strong and tough is simply a matter of not expecting the important things in life to be easy the first time around!

Chapter 6: Galileo and the bravery to stand alone

Today, Galileo Galilei has become something of a secular "martyr for science" due to his moral stance in the face of persecution. But in his time, Galileo faced unthinkable condemnation and adversity. We have considered several inspiring achievements and the exemplary men behind them, but in this chapter, we'll take a look at a personal battle so epic it has arguably not been matched ever since.

The story begins around 1609, when Italian polymath (i.e. master at physics, mathematics, astronomy and engineering) Galileo Galilei became interested in special optical instruments and lenses that allowed for magnified vision. After hearing about work done in Holland, he set to work creating his own rudimentary microscope that could magnify an image 30 times. He also used what he learnt to create a telescope that allowed him to look far out into the heavens and observe the planets and stars.

In time, Galileo made many astonishing discoveries. He saw ridges and valleys on the surface of the moon and stars that were not visible to the naked eye. He realized that the milky way was actually comprised of stars, Jupiter had 4 moons, and he began to learn new and interesting things about the way the planets – including earth – moved through space.

At this point in history, a few other scientists had made similar observations, but it was Galileo who was beginning to put the pieces together and see what all this data implied. At the time, using an instrument that allowed for observation beyond the limits of the human senses was ground-breaking enough, but Galileo's observations eventually led him to conclusions that would not only turn his own life upside down, but completely rock the foundations that his world had been built on.

By 1633, Galileo had been persecuted for his contributions to the theory of heliocentrism, i.e. the scientific model that places the sun at the center of the solar system, with the other planets orbiting around it. But let's rewind to 1610, when, inspired by his observations and experiments, he was moved to publish a work called *Sidereus Nuncius*, translated as "Starry Messenger." In this work, he supported the 1543 work by astronomer Nicolaus Copernicus, *De revolutionibus orbium coelestium*.

To understand what happened next, we need to appreciate that Galileo was not just making scientific claims – he was challenging the conception of what lay at the center of the universe – literally. This was an epic battle between religious dogma and the emerging discoveries of the growing science of astronomy. The Catholic Church held that the Earth was at the center of creation, and according to scripture, if undermined, would seriously threaten their ideological dominance. Their geocentric worldview was not just about the position of heavenly bodies – it was a complex, all-encompassing vision of how the universe was put together and man's rightful place in it.

When Galileo suggested that the Earth was not the center of everything, he was saying so much more: he was asserting his moral rights as a scientist over the religious rulers of the day, he was directly challenging biblical scripture, and he was suggesting something even more frightening: that man was actually nothing special in the grand scheme of things, and that in a complex universe, man was perhaps less significant than he would have liked.

Consider for example that the church would have taught the story contained in Joshua 10:12-13, where God is said to have stopped the motion of the sun so as to lengthen daylight hours and help Joshua lead the Israelites to victory before it grew dark. If Galileo was claiming that this didn't make any sense, and that it is in fact the *earth* that is moving, not the sun, then he would have been implying that the Bible was an unreliable source or, even worse, God himself or his emissaries had lied, misrepresented the truth, or simply not known themselves. Rather than concede the unthinkable, the church announced that Galileo was not only a fraud but a danger to society. His worked was formally declared heresy by the church. Through the period between 1610 to his death in 1642, controversy found Galileo and never left him.

Galileo continued to publish his findings, continued to speak out about what he knew was the truth, and continued to ask further questions that his intellect, and the scientific method, allowed him to answer. Copernicus had also faced opposition, but it was different: he proposed the theory of heliocentrism based on theoretical arguments and logic. Galileo, however, brought concrete evidence to the table: he devised a tool that could directly observe and quantify data that supported Copernicus' initial conjectures.

To make matters worse, Galileo refused to back down. He claimed that the bible is not a scientific authority, and that his work should not be judged wrong because it contradicted bible passages. At the time, this would have been interpreted as breathtaking arrogance and sacrilege – almost akin to claiming that you knew better than God. The scientist was warned continually and in the strongest terms to cease his inquiries and to soften his claims.

Galileo's insistence set off debate all across the world, and the controversy raged on. The fight was messier than it appears at first glance. Galileo made claims but also said that many of his observations were not conclusive, and there were in fact many scientific inconsistencies – which were seized by the church to discredit him. There was plenty of genuine counterevidence for heliocentrism at the time, and so even Galileo's scientific peers were conflicted. The Galileo affair unfolded over decades – which is how long you would expect the complete restructuring of ideology to take! Some members of the church supported him while some scientists condemned him. An elaborate smear campaign of myths and rumors attacked him and his credibility in countless creative ways. His work set off a long, complex, and heavily polarizing shift in society that is, in some ways, still unfolding today.

Eventually, in 1633, the Roman inquisition tried Galileo and found him guilty of heresy. He was sentenced to remain in his home for the rest of his life – which would turn out to be around 9 more years. The ending of the story is not a happy one. By the time Galileo died, heliocentrism had successfully been stamped out as a theory, and his life's work and publications were banned and suppressed. There was immense social pressure not to defend this view or even to acknowledge it.

For a time, Pope Urban VIII had been congenial to Galileo and continued to act as his patron – but on the condition that he always treat the Copernican theory of heliocentrism as a mere hypothesis and not something that could genuinely undermine the church's authority. Naturally, this is not how science works, and in 1632, a year before he was tried and condemned, the Pope severed his patronage officially.

It's important to note that Galileo, essentially, did not triumph in his lifetime. He didn't make some suitably compelling argument and best his enemies. But perhaps this is what makes his quiet determination all the more valuable – he held to it anyway. He fought bravely against ignorance and pressure but did eventually capitulate and recant his claims.

Historians now know that Galileo suffered immensely at the hands of his persecutors, who worked diligently to unravel and discredit everything we was trying so hard to create. Today, people marvel at "cancel culture" and how easy it is to derail a person's entire career for saying the wrong thing. But this is just the tiniest fraction of what Galileo faced. Can you imagine living in a world where expressing your scientific findings leads to the highest authorities in the land denouncing you and condemning you to house arrest for almost a decade?

It took a long, long time for public opinion to change and for scientists gradually to realize the truth of Galileo's claims. The shift took place slowly, as more and more data lent support to the only credible conclusion: the earth really did move around the sun, and many of the dozens of other claims Galileo had made had scientific value. It took a whopping 359 years for the church to acknowledge their mistake and wrongdoing formally, when Pope John Paul II apologized for the injustice of the Galileo affair.

Of course, by this time, the apology meant little – today, we live in the very world that the Catholic Church was seeking to prevent in suppressing Galileo's claims, and now almost nobody holds the worldview they were trying to preserve. Today, our attitudes towards tradition and scientific innovation are exactly reversed – with thanks in part to Galileo's influence.

It's hard to comprehend the cultural and social implications of what unfolded around Galileo's time, and there are few neat and easy accounts of his story. What we can see, however, is that Galileo was a man of singular resilience and grit. Many of us like to think of ourselves as courageous freethinkers, but are we really? How many of us are blindly accepting of what is considered obviously true today – ideas that will mystify and shame our descendants in 300 years' time? In other words, how many Galileos do we have languishing in our midst right now? Do we have the wisdom to know who they are and the courage to stand with them? To perhaps even *be* them?

Galileo was a scientist, but he was more than that: he teaches us about the power and dignity of holding onto what you know is right, even in the face of significant resistance and condemnation. Galileo wasn't exactly a moral crusader, however. He wasn't arguing for his opinion. He frequently expressed uncertainty in some of his own theories and never claimed to be infallible. He never said, "I am 100% right, and I will shout it from the rooftops." Instead, his fight was for the *freedom and entitlement to speak* and to challenge the predominating worldview at the time. It was this, and not arrogance or unbridled conviction that allowed him to continue to speak, despite being suppressed at every turn.

In this way, he had something in common with others on our list – Sanders, Edison, and Beethoven, for example. They all had *something* within them that gave them an inner strength and gravitas. They set their course, they acted as they knew they must, and very little deterred them. Yes, Galileo did officially recant his views, but this does nothing to invalidate his decades of work towards the cause he knew in his conscience was worthwhile.

When we choose a path that is worthy, we often find that it is bigger than our critics, our enemies, our saboteurs. The right path will even be bigger than our own fears and self-doubt. Galileo teaches us that resilience can come from anchoring yourself to a mission in life that is bigger than you. Petty ego concerns, public pressure, fashion, and passing fears can all make us fickle and changeable, but if we have sunk our teeth into a goal that really matters, it is so much harder to shake us loose from it. In fact, we might even be inspired by any resistance we encounter, doubly convinced in the value of us pushing on despite it all.

If you want to be resilient, pick a worthy goal of the largest size you can imagine. Commit yourself to a path that you genuinely believe in, down to your bones. Going with the flow of other people's opinions is easy, but it won't make you resilient or robust. Being an authentic individual with your own moral and intellectual code is less easy, but it will fortify you and make any setback easier to endure.

Today, many people assume the story of Galileo is a simple one about science vs. religion, but it's more than that – after all, Galileo remained a Catholic and man of faith all his life, despite being a dedicated scientist. He said, "I do not feel obliged to believe that the same God who has endowed us with sense, reason, and intellect has intended us to forgo their use." Galileo's commitment was to the project of inquiry itself, to sense, reason, and intellect.

He was able to endure because he saw his project as going beyond his own ego and immediate interests. Like other noteworthy figures in history, he used his own will and intelligence to grasp the world around him, rather than have others decide what he should think and why. Galileo was able to speak against the church because he served something bigger than it; is there something in your life that you serve that is bigger than the political and historical period you inhabit?

"Philosophy [nature] is written in that great book whichever is before our eyes -- I mean the universe -- but we cannot understand it if we do not first learn the language and grasp the symbols in which it is written." If you are, like Galileo was, busy with the work of reading the great book of the universe, then of course you are resilient – what could the petty squabbling and criticisms from others matter to you then?

Real world example:

Marilyn vos Savant was a real life genius and prodigy who held the Guinness world record for the highest IQ. She penned a famous magazine column called *Ask Marilyn* in which she answered readers' tricky questions. One day, Marilyn was asked about the notoriously thorny Monty Hall problem, which was a probability puzzle that had stumped mathematicians for years. Marilyn gave her answer.

What followed was relentless criticism and mockery from all corners of academia. Learned people flocked to call her an idiot for not arriving at the then-popular interpretation, and she received thousands of letters saying the same thing: she was wrong.

It turns out that Marilyn was right. After years of name-calling, misogyny, and academic persecution, it gradually became clear that Marilyn had simply seen beyond the problem and solved it more elegantly than her persecutors could understand at the time. Fortunately for Marilyn, though, some of her fiercest critics did apologize, and she was vindicated.

Galileo Galilei's lessons:

- Be true to yourself. Have faith in your own judgment and stick to your firmly held convictions, even if you have to do

so alone. This will imbue you with enormous courage and resilience in the face of challenges, because you will believe in yourself.
- Be humble. Use your intellect and your reason to the best of your ability, but always be willing to learn more. Don't boast about your conclusions but allow them to guide your convictions quietly from within. If you're lost, stay curious and return to the faculties that you're blessed with – keep asking questions and be brave enough to discover the answers.
- Realize that, sadly, you will not always be rewarded for your diligence and persistence. Instead, seek to find meaning and purpose in your work, whatever it is, so that it inspires you even if nobody else recognizes its value. Then, you will have tapped a well of strength that very few will be able to match!

Chapter 7: The battle of Zama: The Roman's secret to winning

We now turn our attention from musical genius, literature, and high adventure to the world of the Roman Empire. In fact, in the time our story takes place, Rome was not yet an empire but a republic governed by consuls. At the time, Rome had fought several battles with Carthage, and in one noteworthy war, the Carthaginian General Hannibal advanced on the Romans, winning a series of important battles that racked up more than 100,000 casualties.

In the biggest and most notable of the Punic war battles, the battle of Cannae in 216 B.C., Hannibal used a novel military strategy that impressed scholars and historians for decades afterwards. It is still regarded as one of the best military plays in history. Basically, Hannibal pretended to have a weak and undefended center, and when the Roman army took the bait, so to speak, Hannibal's troops wrapped around them on all sides and encircled them.

The Romans responded as best they could but were viciously defeated by Hannibal. But, this story is not about Hannibal and his military accomplishments, which were many. It's not about his superior cunning in Cannae that day. Rather, this is a story about the losers of this war – the Romans. Their story is one that goes to show that being defeated is not the end.

To skip to the end of the story, a few years later in 202 B.C., Hannibal was finally defeated by the Romans at the battle of Zama (in present-day Tunisia), led by Scipio Africanus the Elder. It took some time for them to make their comeback, but the Romans got their revenge, and in 146 B.C., all of Carthage was destroyed. A hundred years after that, Rome would become a powerful empire, and their renewed vigor came in large part from their astounding retaliation after Cannae.

So how exactly did they come back from such a defeat? To understand what was so important about both the loss at Cannae and the battles that followed and to see what this ancient military event could teach us about resilience, we need to understand what war was like in those days. Kings would typically take their armies to a battlefield and square off directly, one army against another. It was brutal. The troops would fight, and the winner would take all after killing the opponent or forcing their surrender. It's like chess: the war is over when one team is checkmated.

The bloodshed that unfolded at Cannae was something most people today cannot envision. The Carthaginians *slaughtered* the Romans, and the fields ran with their blood. Roman historian Titus Livius (or Livy) claimed that, "Some were discovered lying there alive, with thighs and tendons slashed, baring their necks and throats and bidding their conquerors drain the remnant of their blood. Others were found with their heads buried in holes dug in the ground. They had apparently made these pits for themselves, and heaping the dirt over their faces shut off their breath." For a Roman soldier, nothing mattered more than service to the republic, honor to their families, and the courage to uphold the national Roman spirit. Defeat was so unthinkable that suicide was a preferable option.

Around 50,000 to 70,000 Romans had been cut down this way and thousands more captured. It was a humiliating defeat that sent shock waves through Rome. Despite the Romans having a larger army, Hannibal had prevailed with superior strategy and lost just 6000 men. Back home, the families of the Roman soldiers wailed in the streets and even conducted human sacrifices in their desperate attempt to appease the gods and spare them from their enemies. It was a republic on the brink of collapse. Try to imagine the scale: seven times as many men were lost in one day at Cannae as had been killed in the battle of Gettysburg. It was a national disaster.

Yet the public was told to limit their mourning to 30 days. Though the Romans were defeated, they refused to give up. After the 30 days of national mourning, there were to be no more tears. The senate in Rome flatly refused any peace offerings from Hannibal and would not pay any ransom for prisoners taken at Cannae. Instead, they got to work planning.

Every citizen was put to work making weapons. The debilitated army was pieced back together again by lowering the recruitment age and enlisting convicts and even slaves who were promised freedom if they fought for Rome. They would return to Cannae, and they would return stronger.

Rome had nearly been annihilated in one of the biggest battles in history … but they weren't out of the game yet. Hannibal had been an audacious and formidable enemy, who had managed to lead his army to rampage across the countryside, destroying legions of Roman soldiers, but the Romans would simply have to do better.

Initially, in retaliation, they attacked supply lines supporting Hannibal's army, avoiding the kind of "pitched battles" that Hannibal was an expert at waging. But this was just a stalling tactic. They soon elected Gaius Terentius Varro and Lucius Aemilius Paullus as co-consuls and gathered together their new army – the largest the republic had ever seen. They marched into southern Italy and seized a supply depot near Cannae. Hannibal had 40,000 infantry and 10,00 cavalries (and, sadly, far fewer war elephants, since many had now died).

The Romans, on the other hand, came with 80,000 troops and 6000 cavalries.

Scipio Africanus the Elder, leading what must have been the most epic comeback mission of living memory, had under his command several Roman soldiers who had been thrashed at the battle of Cannae and were now looking to redeem themselves. The Roman soldiers were now far superior in training and number – plus they had something to prove.

Hannibal may have won the previous battle with a flourish of impressive tactics, but his army was now considerably spent – the men were tired, their resources were dwindling, and even the horses had been killed at the time to stop the Romans from seizing them. On top of this, Hannibal and his troops responded late to the new threat advancing on them, leaving Scipio to choose the site to their advantage. While Hannibal had seemed to have so sure an upper hand, his advantage had all but evaporated in a flurry of poor planning.

According to Livy, Hannibal reportedly said to Scipio, "What I was years ago at Trasimene and Cannae, you are today." And he was right. Scipio had the advantage of well-trained, driven troops who arranged themselves into maniples, which were impenetrable infantry units. Though war elephants seem like a formidable enemy, in reality, they were not trained enough to attack in a coordinated, flexible way and ended up causing more chaos than they were worth. The innovative maniple layout allowed the troops to clump together and form gulleys down which the elephants ran to avoid them, passing through harmlessly. Some elephants, frightened by the trumpeting, ended up crushing their own cavalry. The Roman troops unleashed an attack that was swift and powerful, crushing every line of attack the Carthaginians could muster.

Hannibal's men found that they weren't fighting the same army that they had triumphed over in Cannae. Instead, they saw men that were toughened, smarter, and filled with fire. What's more, they were now familiar with the tactics that had beat them once before. Hannibal's men were exhausted and overwhelmed. Around 20,000 of them died in that battle, with perhaps the same again held captive. The Romans, however, lost only 1500.

Carthage was decimated and surrendered to Scipio, ceding to the Romans' demands and offering up their warships to be publicly burnt. Rome set an indemnity payment from Carthage of 10,000 talents, which was more than three times the size of the indemnity claimed at the end of the first Punic war, so many years prior. Hannibal himself fled and was not seen in Carthage for many years and never again commanded in battle. For his victory, Scipio was awarded the title of "Africanus" to commemorate a glorious new era in the empire. Hannibal was a formidable enemy, and by defeating him, Rome asserted its supremacy as uncontested master of parts of Africa, Spain, and the Hellenistic East.

Today, historians see this final Punic battle as the one that cemented Rome's new reign and ended the sovereignty of Carthage forevermore. From there, Rome could increase control over the Mediterranean and, in leaps and bounds, build their empire. What we see in this story is that, even if you are an accomplished leader like Hannibal and pull off the perfect example of military annihilation on your foes, they may be even more determined to come back again and win once and for all.

What can we learn from this epic saga of triumph after defeat? Are we to conclude that Hannibal did something wrong and that Scipio was somehow smarter? No. After all, years on, Hannibal was given his own statue in the Roman pantheon of admirable military commanders and admired for his efforts. He was, after all, a worthy adversary that had inspired the Romans to step up and be more than anyone thought they could be.

What we can see from this chapter in history, however, is the power of not only refusing to be defeated but using loss and failure to *inspire you to be even better*. The Roman republic could have fallen back, sunk into self-pity, and spent the next few decades licking its wounds. But it didn't. There was public acknowledgment of the agony and anguish that the loss at Cannae had caused , but this was limited. After the tears were dried, there was work to do.

What the classical heroes of old can show us is that *action* can be an amazing healer. After your world comes to pieces, you might not know what to do with yourself. In each of our lives, we have to face the personal and psychological equivalent of the battle of Cannae – the death of a loved one, divorce, financial ruin, a serious health scare or accident, natural disasters, trauma or all of these. Many times, we are bested by someone or something that shines genuine light on our flaws – we might discover that we have underestimated a challenge or that we're paying dearly for our foolishness.

Either way, the Romans' response to Cannae is a powerful example. Don't dwell too long on what has been lost. Mourn, but let it be limited – instead, empower yourself by making plans. If things didn't go your way, don't get mired in blame, victimhood, or self-pity. Instead, ask honestly what went wrong and how you can be better next time. "Don't get mad, get even," comes to mind. The Romans weren't just mourning their loss of the thousands of troops. They were mourning the attack to their identity as a powerful and capable republic. It was a matter of pride.

Sure, you don't want to be driven by your ego alone, but if you can channel any sense of wounded pride into some *useful action*, then you allow yourself to get back up and continue fighting. The Romans never cried foul or played victim. They had been beaten, fair and square, and they allowed the sobering realization of their defeat to energize them, not demoralize them. As a commander, Hannibal had acted commendably. Instead of belittling his fair achievement, they would rise to his level – and higher.

If you want a masterclass in resilience, take a page from the Romans' attitude during this period. Don't be a sore loser, ever. They may have been severely crushed in battle and had both their pride and their nation left in tatters, but this did not undermine their dignity. They pulled together the resources they had, they planned and strategized, they worked hard, and they came back again, ten times stronger than before.

Scipio, it turns out, did not have a glittering military career for too long after the glorious triumph at Zama, and he died young. Rather, it was the Roman people's spirit of persistence, bravery, and discipline that acted as the real hero in this story. The "secret to winning" is not somehow to find a way never to lose. The Romans lost. *Badly*. But that loss wasn't the last thing they did. In fact, losing was precisely what allowed them to double down and come back even better than before.

Losing is only a true loss if you accept it as the final word and give up. If you lose but choose to learn, to grow, to be stronger than you were before, then it is not really a loss at all but a cherished lesson. Some people think that, to be resilient, you need to forgive the past, forget it, and move on. This may be true for some, but for the Romans, their path to reclaiming their power was to hold onto the past and use it inspire and drive them to something better.

Your failures don't define you. *How you respond to them* does. The entire fate of the Western world was changed forever that day in Zama. Individually and collectively, the Romans made a decision that they would not agree to be defined as losers. They would rewrite their story the way *they* wanted, and if that meant that they had to create an army more sophisticated than any they had had before, then so be it – that's what they would do. How much sweeter the victory when you know how much it cost you to rise to the challenge of winning that victory!

Everyday example

Imagine Chris, who's always dreamt of a glittering music career – or at least recognition for his talents. One day, after years of finetuning his craft, he books a gig where he is fully intending to blow away the audience with his novel musical style. On the night, he completely flops. The crowd hates it, and near the end of his set, he even gets booed and hurried along off the stage. It's a crushing blow to his self-esteem, and late that evening, he is in full despair, vowing to give up forever and never try again.

In the morning, however, he wakes up with a different view on things. As much as it pains him to admit it, the audience was right: he can see now that he has a lot to learn and needs to go back to the drawing board. Not letting his wounded ego get the better of him for too long, he is soon practicing again and shrugging off the embarrassment. It takes him almost 5 more years before he tries again – but when he does, the crowd really is blown away. Inwardly, he thanks all those people who booed him the first time around. It was harsh, but it taught him something that he might not have learnt otherwise – *to be better.*

Scipio and the Roman army's lessons:

- Don't give up. Failure, loss, and disappointment are not the end of the line. Learn, try again, and do better the next time around. Have the courage to accept what can be improved and, instead of dwelling on the pain of your defeat, get proactive and start *doing*.
- It's cowardly to blame others for your shortcomings or to get angry at life in general for not being fair. If you've been justly beaten, accept it graciously. Don't be a bad loser. In fact, if you can, try to welcome even painful challenges in life as an opportunity to learn and be better. Like the Romans, we can all build monuments to those who have taught us our most difficult lessons.

- Hard work is a wonderful remedy for pain and loss. Resilience is not just about passively accepting your lot – you can empower yourself by taking action, and this will make any hardship 100 times easier to bear.

Chapter 8: Alexander the Great and the land bridge to Tyre Island

Speaking of great men, our list wouldn't be complete unless we included a historical figure with "great" in his very name. The further back in history we go, the harder it is to find accurate, neutral, and detailed accounts of the personalities of great leaders, thinkers, or rulers, but we can certainly infer a lot by examining their choices and actions.

Let's take a look at a story of Alexander the Great and a small city called Tyre that was founded in around 2750 BC. The city was on an island, and on the mainland was another settlement called Ushu. Tyre was, from a strategic perspective, an important commercial seaport, and throughout ancient history, it was invaded and controlled in turn by basically every European culture that surrounded it at the time.

In 332 BC, Alexander the Great, who was hellbent on conquering nothing less than the entire world, set his eyes on Tyre. His historic campaign from Macedonia had already left a string of subjugated towns and villages in his wake. Then he got to Tyre. This was a problem – how would he invade and subdue a city on an island?

It was easy work to take the mainland city of Ushu. But he was stumped about how to manage Tyre. There was no question of moving on without occupying the island, since this would expose his armies to ambush from the rear as they advanced. Now, if you think that this story is going to be one in which we discover the impressive military and strategic skill of Alexander, you'd be wrong: this is a story about impressive *engineering* feats.

Today, geological scientists and historians have worked hard to examine the area today (the city is now called Sour) and study the landscape to try recreating what it was that Alexander and his army were facing at the time. The scientists realized that, in Alexander's time, there would have been, lying a few meters under sea level, the answer to their problem: a narrow sandbar joining Tyre Island to the mainland.

Over the course of seven long and hard months, Alexander's formidable war machine set out to create a path to the island on top of this sandbar.

They piled up stone, timber, and whatever rubble they could find to raise the sandbar above sea level so it could be walked on. This would have been an astonishing 220 feet in width alone. Considering the technology available at the time (hint: it was basically nothing), this achievement was especially striking.

As it happened, the sandbar plan wasn't the main reason that Alexander was eventually able to lay siege to the city and claim it. But the skills the army developed were used again later on, when the same tactic was employed to create a bridge from the Egyptian mainland to the Island of Pharos.

Most fascinating of all, though, is the longer term impact this land bridge made on the landscape. The bridge they built acted as a barrier against which silt slowly accumulated, until it created the 700,000 square feet of new land now in the area. Aerial photos show that Tyre Island is not much of an island anymore and is connected by a broad peninsula to the mainland. It is incredible to imagine that an army, led by a single man, was responsible for altering the very face of the earth. Alexander the Great only lived to 32 years of age and never did achieve world domination as he had hoped. But today, thousands of years after his death, the land still shows the mark of the siege of Tyre.

Plenty has been written about Alexander the Great. His full appellation was Alexander III of Macedon, and he was born in 356 BC, succeeding his father Phillip II as the king of the ancient Greek realm of Macedon. He succeeded his father, who was assassinated at the wedding of Cleopatra of Macedon (no, not that Cleopatra), and though just 20 years old when made king, he spent more or less all of his career on a vast military campaign to conquer Asia and Northeast Africa – and then later, the known world. Through Alexander, one of history's most immense empires was created, and he is still remembered today as being unbeaten in battle.

If Alexander the Great seems to you to be a figure of almost mythical, non-human proportions, this is for a reason. He was tutored by the great Aristotle ("I am indebted to my father for living, but to my teacher for living well") and was known to be a military genius the likes of which the world had never seen. It's hard to imagine how he had achieved so many noteworthy battles sieges and invasions at the age of just 30. He is a man who had 20 cities named after him (one, for example, is Alexandria in Egypt).

Alexander is responsible for the spread of Greek culture, which morphed in time into Hellenistic civilization, out of which sprung the Roman Empire and the Western world we can recognize as such today. From the time of his death, every military leader of note would forever be compared to the gold standard that Alexander set. Military academies still admire and teach his distinctive tactics and strategies today.

There are also plenty of other quasi-legends about the leader's childhood and private life. Plutarch related that, on her wedding night, Alexander's mother Olympias dreamt that a bolt of lightning struck her womb and spread a flame that covered the entire world. His father, Philip II, was also reported to have prophetic dreams about his soon-to-be son: he saw a vision of himself putting a royal seal on Olympias's womb with the image of a lion. Ambitious Olympias is said to have believed literally and seriously in her son's greatness, reportedly teaching him from an early age that he was in fact the son of Zeus and more than a mere mortal. Considering that her marriage to Phillip was merely a political one and that she resented her husband, we can understand why she might have convinced the boy that his real father was in fact a god.

On the day Alexander was born, his father received news of an auspicious victory in the kingdom and simultaneously that one of the 7 wonders of the world, the Temple of Artemis, had burnt down. Alexander was raised like any other noble Macedonian youth: he received a classical education and was taught to ride horses, hunt, fight, read, and play the lyre. Even as a youth, people recognized his vaulting ambition. After his epic but surprisingly short military career, Alexander died at just 32 from causes not yet fully determined – possibly alcohol, typhoid fever, or poisoning by his enemies.

While all of this pomp and grandeur is certainly interesting, it's hard to imagine what a man that lived thousands of years ago could teach us about resilience, grit, and determination today. The world that Alexander lived in was very different from ours. He was born into luxury and privilege that most of us would associate with only the wealthiest celebrities today, yet he was also ostracized by his own court and, being ruler of the weakest kingdom, generally despised by the Greeks. There was even a time when Alexander and his mother were exiled from the kingdom because of political disagreements over Philip's subsequent son – the rightful heir, since Alexander could not be, being only half-Macedonian.

Alexander thus had a potent combination of two quite different experiences: the shame of being a "half-blood" and second in line to his younger brother, who would be king, but also the deeply held conviction that he was in truth destined for greatness. It doesn't take a psychologist to see that Alexander had an immense chip on his shoulder and would spend his entire life emphatically proving himself and his identity and searching for a place to call home. Can you imagine a person like this, being made ruler of several vast and powerful kingdoms all over the world, including Egypt, where was he was deemed a pharaoh and thus of divine origin? It's hard to picture a time in history when men worshipped rulers not merely as kings but as literal embodiments of divinities, but this is the world that Alexander lived in.

By the time he arrived at Tyre, then, he was already a formidable military force and believed completely in his title as the greatest living general to grace the earth and probably a god as well. What could us mere mortals learn from this man who lived so extraordinary a life that it's hard to believe some of it is true? Are we supposed to conclude that monstrous narcissism and relentless aggression is what makes a person "great"?

No, probably not. But Alexander the Great does show us just how much is possible when innate talent is paired with opportunity and a rock-solid self-belief. Try to put yourself in the mind of Alexander, who regularly took actions that affected not just hundreds of thousands of people in his own country, but hundreds of thousands more in far-off, exotic lands that most people could scarcely imagine, let alone conquer. Picture the sense of self-control, the size of his vision, and the gargantuan self-confidence it would have taken to believe genuinely that conquering the entire world was not only possible, but you had a plan to do it. And that plan was working.

This gives us an insight into why Alexander acted as he did when it came to seizing Tyre. He saw an obstacle and found a way around it. The fact that his solution required thousands of men and several months' work was irrelevant. He did it. When the landscape was not amenable to his plans, *he changed the landscape.*

So sure was his will and so certain was his determination to get what he wanted that he undertook a plan that had been unthinkable until then in military history. What's interesting is that, in Tyre, Alexander proved that he was not just a military genius. He was a genius, period, and he was willing to do whatever it took to achieve his goals, whether that meant battle tactics or overseeing an audacious engineering project that modern builders would even balk at today.

We cannot exactly call Alexander's response to the problem of Tyre "adversity," and we cannot frame his novel solution as an instance of resilience or overcoming adversity. Rather, we can see in Alexander's life that we need never frame anything standing in our way as an "obstacle" at all. It is merely something that we have yet to bend to our will. While an excellent but conventional military strategist might have thought, "Hm, this is difficult – how could you lay siege to an *island*?" the Great Alexander simply decided, "We will have to make it so that it's not an island anymore!"

What could *you* achieve if you had even a fraction of the bombast and arrogance that Alexander did? How would you behave if the world knew your name, and that name was routinely affixed with "The Great"? Chances are, you'd take a lot more risks, feel a lot more secure in yourself... and crucially, face adversity in a completely new way. You may not even see it as adversity.

In the modern world, many of us get overly attached to a kind of victim mentality and may create narratives for ourselves in which we are hard done by, set back, or unfairly treated by others or life itself. It's as though we are the opposite of Alexander the Great – instead, we walk around as though we were *Michael the Puny* or *Jenny the Weak*. When we encounter a difficulty, we panic. Even though we may not frame it this way, it can feel like life, like the gods themselves are standing in our way. But if you are Alexander the Great, you *are* a god. You are in charge. You can never be a victim, only an active agent. You decide. You identify your course and take action until it's achieved. You are not at anyone's mercy, and even when you face uncertainty, suffering, loss or defeat, even this does nothing to reduce your dignity or self-belief.

"I would rather excel others in the knowledge of what is excellent, than in the extent of my powers and domination," said Alexander. For this great man, his strength and conviction came from striving for the good, the noble, the virtuous. Despite being rightly viewed as a bloodthirsty warlord by many, he was also determined that every subject in his kingdom would be an equal, regardless of station, creed, or color. At the end of his life, he was believed to have said, "A tomb now suffices him for whom the whole world was not sufficient."

Everyday example

Melissa would never consider herself to have anything in common with Alexander the Great, but she shares in his mindset when she decides one day to pursue her dream, no matter what. Melissa dreams of working for a company she's admired from afar for years. But with little formal education and being a single mother to two young children, there's no way she could work there, even if by some miracle she convinced them to hire her.

So she takes an alternative route. Melissa strategizes and first angles for a lowly *cleaning job* at the company and, after being hired, gradually convinces management to let her implement a progressive childcare center on site and be in charge of its operation. Impressed with her competence and vision, the same management soon agrees to mentor Melissa and give her career advice. Within a few short years, the perfect job opens up in the company – and Melissa has made sure she's first to apply and top of mind with the bosses, who already know and like her. The best part? She now works at a company that provides onsite childcare.

In other words, when she couldn't reach Tyre, she built a bridge!

Alexander the Great's lessons:

- When facing an obstacle, don't get despondent or give up – simply become curious about **how** you will get around it (take the fact that you will get around it as a foregone conclusion!)
- Believe in yourself. No need to be a megalomaniac of Alexander the Great proportions, but don't allow others to tell you what you are and are not capable of doing. This, rather than self-pity and feeling victimized, can bless you with far more dignity and resilience.
- If your plans aren't working, change the plans. If the story takes a bad turn, change the story. If you're losing the game, change the rules of the game until you are winning! The most successful people in history didn't wait to be given

permission to believe in their own competence – they just barged ahead and believed it anyway.

Chapter 9: Julius Caesar and the battle of Alesia

Let's turn our attention back to antiquity and explore the story of Julius Caesar and the battle of Alesia. The event we'll look at it is widely considered one of Caesar's most impressive military victories, but on its face, the odds appeared entirely against him, at first. Though it is an extraordinary example of war strategy, we can also see in this story a powerful allegory for approaching difficulties in our lives.

Let's set the scene. It's September in 52 BC, and the Gallic wars are underway. The Gallic wars were a series of campaigns led by Julius Caesar against the people in Gaul, which is a region now roughly around France and Belgium. Though historians mainly have Caesar's own account of the wars to go on (his book *Commentarii de Bello Gallico*), we do have other sources to help us confirm the casualty numbers and the series of events as they unfolded.

One of the most noteworthy battles was in the small settlement of Alesia, the capital of the Mandubii. The location of this town would be significant – it was perched high on a hill. Intending to seize the regions in Gaul for farmland, Caesar had been in the area since 58 BC, attempting to "pacify" the region and bring it under complete Roman control. Tribe after tribe was subjugated, often brutally, and the lands were ravaged. When he left the region, he ensured that no grain supplies would reach the survivors, so they would starve.

The Gauls united and rose up against Caesar, and the brave warrior Vercingetorix, King of the Averni, was an important leading figure, who drew the scattered tribes together to defend themselves. In response to this, the Romans redoubled their efforts, and a wave of bloodshed and violence spread over the region for many years. Caesar had his work cut out for him in pursuing Vercingetorix, and the battles raged on, with minor victories going to each side. Finally, however, Vercingetorix retreated the entire army to a small walled town on a hill – Alesia.

Now, according to Caesar, the metrics of the battle that would ensue were as follows:

On the Gaul's side:

80,000 men in Alesia and 100,000 to 250,000 men in relief army, all led by Vercingetorix and two other commanders who would join later, Commius and Vercassivellaunus.

On Rome's side:

60,000 men, led by Julius Caesar.

It would appear that Caesar would be entering into a game that he had slim hope of winning. What was worse is that Alesia had a perfectly strategic location. Perched on hill surrounded by river valleys, it was ideally situated to defend itself against attackers, but Caesar made a decision that would transform this seeming disadvantage into an advantage. He could not defeat the enemy's army because they were so numerous and neatly encircled all in one place. On the other hand, how convenient would it be if the army was neatly encircled, all in one place...?

All of Vercingetorix's army was within those walls – that could be seen as a problem, or it could be seen as an extremely lucky break. The goal, then, was not to attack from the front, where Vercingetorix's army would just pick off the Romans one by one. Rather, Caesar instructed his army to build a wall (like Alexander the Great's men at Tyre Island, they must have marveled at how often soldiers are asked to also be builders and engineers!). The Romans built a fortification that is known as a circumvallation, which comes from the Latin *circumvallare,* which means to circle around *("circum") and rampart ("vallum").* This rampart would encircle the entire settlement of Alesia with a series of walls, ditches, trips, and watchtowers all designed to make sure that Alesia could not receive any aid from the outside. The wall, essentially, made the settlement's defensive position into a liability.

Of course, a wall takes time to build, and Vercingetorix guessed Caesar's intentions and launched several attacks to try to prevent the Romans from completing their work. Not only were Caesar's men able to fend them off, but they managed to finish the rampart in just three weeks. Considering that the entire construction was ten miles long and included 24 separate watchtowers, this was certainly no mean feat. Behind the wall, the men dug three six-meter-deep trenches, even filling the last one with river water. Stakes were sharpened and stuck into the ground as further deterrents. There were even eight rows of hidden pits in which thick, sharps stakes had been set up below, ready to impale the man who tried to escape. The Gauls were going nowhere.

And now, since Caesar knew that the people inside would continue to attempt escape, he set to work on building *another* fortress, encircling the first. After all, a few escapees had already breached the walls and disappeared. This rampart, however, was armed facing the other direction, not inwards to keep the Gaul tribes in, but also outwards to keep out any aid that the escapees might bring with them. This wall was called a contravallation – a counter rampart.

This was bad news for the people inside, who gradually began to starve. Trapped inside, conditions deteriorated fast. Once rationed food was exhausted, cannibalism was even suggested. In a tragic turn, the Gauls and Alesians decided to release the women, children, sick, and elderly, hoping Caesar would show them mercy, take them, and feed them. He did not. These people were left in between the two walls, and as they braved the elements and starved to death, it drastically lowered the morale of the men still inside the town.

As predicted, help did eventually arrive, even as Vercingetorix was considering surrender. At the end of September, there was a coordinated attack on both walls from the outside and the inside, and when this failed, another attempt under the cover of night.

It was October the 2nd that things reached boiling point, and 60,000 Gauls led by Vercassivellaunus launched an attack against a weak point in the rampart. The ensuing battles was vicious and protracted, but by the next day, Vercingetorix surrendered, saying that his men should either kill him there and then or offer him alive as a kind of tribute to Caesar. His men chose to surrender him, and the Romans kept him captive for 6 years more. He was eventually executed.

In the battle of Alesia, the Romans were said to have suffered around 12,800 wounded or killed, with the Gauls reportedly losing up to 250,000, with 40,000 captured. It was a monumental personal victory for Caesar and the infamous siege that put a stop to resistance in Gaul and handed it over to Roman rule. The Roman senate even declared 20 days of thanksgiving.

Now, at first glance, it can be hard to see what life lessons we could glean from this story (other than, perhaps, not to try to resist subjugation by Caesar...). However, studying important events from history can give us insight into a special, practical kind of problem solving that is sometimes difficult to appreciate in your own life – unless you're a celebrated Roman consulate, that is.

What makes military history so interesting is that it is, in many ways, a live chess game that unfolds in unpredictable ways. And often, it is not strength or greater numbers that ensures victory for the winning side, but cunning, innovation and shrewd leadership. Even if you don't plan to lay siege to an ancient Mandubii settlement anytime soon, you almost certainly will have faced a situation in which it felt like the odds were stacked against you. Maybe you've been dealt an unfair disadvantage, you're working with too few resources, or you're "on the back foot," metaphorically speaking.

But in this story we see that, in battle, this isn't the only thing that matters. Like Alexander the Great did with his epic sandbar plan, Caesar took the challenge facing him and turned it on its head. His plan to build two walls trapping his opponents was an entirely new innovation that proved that, when physical prowess might not have been enough, an intelligent, novel solution could be. Guesses vary widely, and it's now considered likely that Caesar exaggerated his own account, but even modest estimates have each Roman pitted against at least two Gauls.

But what Caesar's technique shows us is that, even if things are not quite to your favor, it doesn't mean you are completely without resources or a way out. Whether Caesar's political and military career is inspiring to you or not, and whether you agree with his methods, it's pretty clear that he was a man who knew how to play the cards he was dealt. This was someone who knew exactly what strings to pull to find himself rising in Roman society, and his play at the battle of Alesia is just one of many incidents that give us a peek into this ancient man's mindset.

What characterizes all of Caesar's key historical moments is one thing: his willingness to change the game, to play his own game. Of course, he wasn't reckless or a rebel – first he played by the rules, and then he broke them ("If you must break the law, do it to seize power; in all other cases, observe it"). Many great leaders teach us a similar lesson: before you can turn things upside down, see a fresh perspective, or solve a problem in an innovative way, you need to have a keen, intelligent grasp of facts as they are right now.

Caesar was a politician and knew how to work public opinion in his favor. He knew how to talk to his troops and inspire them to fight for him no matter what. He was ambitious, but he knew when and how to express this ambition, so he ultimately got what he wanted. Caesar is the perfect example of someone who understands tact, diplomacy, and tactics. It wasn't sheer brute force or moral right that won him his many victories – it was cunning. And this cunning rests on the ability of a person to see into the rules of the game being played… and see a way to shift things so they come out on top.

Like Alexander the Great, Caesar had an indefatigable belief in his own entitlement to glory, but he also worked hard to conquer anything that stood in the way of his unfolding vision. In fact, one story goes that Caesar was put in awe of a statue of Alexander the Great when he was around 31 years old. He must have known then that Alexander already had, by that age, achieved immense glory. From that point, he would have redoubled his efforts – as Alexander did, so would he.

Like other ambitious and power-hungry generals and military leaders before and since, Caesar was a potent mix of grandeur, narcissism, and relentless drive, but he was also very, very intelligent. During the battle of Alesia, Caesar showed how he had been playing the game all along – within the rules, but also outside of them, when necessary.

How many of us can be said to possess this kind of strategic sense? How many of us are merely passively reacting to the conditions of our lives instead of asking, "Hang on, what can *I* create here? How can I change this story and play things differently?" Resilience, discipline, and consistency are only the outward signs of a deeper mental condition: the ability to be the authors of our own lives, the creators of our fates. Ultimately, the great men we've uncovered in these pages were so effective at leadership and domination because they were first able to conquer and master *themselves*.

There are many intelligent, strong, and capable people in the world, and certainly many ambitious ones. There are also many people who've been given great opportunities to exploit. But it is a rare talent to *create* those opportunities even when they don't exist. Caesar wasn't always Caesar. The man we know him as today was an image created deliberately and with purposeful effort. Some solutions will require a bit of out-of-the-box thinking, like Caesar showed at Alesia, but others will take a lot longer to play out. Caesar was known, for example, to plant seeds that would take years to yield results. But he followed through, he schemed, he plotted, he planned, and he undertook those plans with the careful precision of a chess-player.

Making the kind of mental shift required to think on the level of a Caesar or an Alexander is obviously no overnight project. But it's easy enough to begin. Simply realize that nothing is set in stone. As long as the game is underway and you're still in it, anything can happen. Even if the chips are down and things are looking bad for you, take a deep breath and remind yourself that it can be changed.

Look at what you are currently considering a disadvantage and see if it can be framed as an advantage. Look at the nature of your attackers and think carefully about the logic of your response to them. There is enormous resilience to be had in the refuge you can take in your own self-mastery. Don't like what's happening? Then change it.

Caesar is rumored to have said, "In war, events of importance are the result of trivial causes," and "Fortune, which has a great deal of power in other matters but especially in war, can bring about great changes in a situation through very slight forces." In other words, it's not over till the fat lady sings! Even small acts and shifts in attitude can impact the great unfolding of fate. Though this means we need never lose hope because things can improve when we least expect it, it also means that we should never get too comfortable with things going our way – our fortune could swiftly change for the worse, too. This is why Caesar, even as he was thrashing the Alesians in their settlement, kept an eye open for those that had escaped, anticipated an attack from them, and prepared accordingly. Caesar never counted on luck, superstition, or charity. He was a leader, and that meant he took full and total responsibility for being the sole arbiter of his own fate.

Everyday example

Michael was an author who was having trouble getting agents to consider his work or convincing publishing houses to consider given his books a second glance. One day, an especially rude publisher tells him, "Look, I think this is the single worst book I've ever read." It's not a fair comment, but it does give Michael a strange new idea...

He gets to work writing something new – something he never considered. He abandons his old manuscripts and changes tack completely. Within a few years, Michael is at the top of bestseller charts after all and raking it in. He's made a name for himself with a self-published book titled *The Worst Book You'll Ever Read*, in which he writes a humorous mock self-help guide teaching his readers how to construct an anti-masterpiece that will have their audience heaving up their lunch. People love it.

Julius Caesar's lessons:

- No matter how bleak things look, stay calm and take heart: you always have the power to choose your response, and you can often turn a disadvantage into an advantage simply by changing your perspective.
- When faced with a challenge or obstacle, try to think outside of the box and imagine a solution beyond your current way of thinking. Understand the rules, like Caesar, and then be brave and audacious enough to rewrite them completely to your advantage.
- There is never any reason for despair or giving up – things can and often do change at a moment's notice. Stay alert and take whatever action you can, reminding yourself that, if there are no opportunities on the table that you like,

you can create opportunities. The double rampart idea didn't exist before the battle of Alesia – what novel solution to your own current problems is just one ingenious idea away?

Chapter 10: The battle of Thermopylae

Have you seen the 2006 film *300* by director Zack Snyder? If you have, you already have some sense of the glory and epic scale of the battle of Thermopylae, on which the movie was based. The film is over-the-top to say the least, and the fantastical elements are dialed up to 11, showing the Greek Spartans, the heroes of the tale, as near godlike in their strength and bravery.

If we're considering noteworthy historical battles that could teach us something true about the human spirit of discipline and resilience, then we surely can't leave out the Spartans and their victory at Thermopylae. The megawatt bravery and violence shown in the film seems unlikely, but just how much of it was really true?

The story (legend, at this point?) goes that just 300 Spartans battled against Persia's infinitely larger army (estimates range from 100,000 to two million) for three long days, when they triumphed spectacularly and went down in history as ultra-warriors the likes of which the world had never seen. Today, historians can agree that there probably were just 300 Spartan men at Thermopylae (which, incidentally, is a name that translates to "Hot Gates" since the Sulphur springs there were in myth reported to be one of the gates to Hell – what a fitting place for an epic battle to unfold!).

It's likely, though, that these 300 were not alone and were assisted by troops from other Greek states with whom they were in alliance (such as the Thebans and Thespians), bringing the real number closer to something like 7000 men. What about the Persians? In the 5th century, Herodotus claimed that they numbered more than 2 million, but scholars think this is unlikely and estimate the number at around 300,000 maximum.

So, even if the details of the battle itself were slightly exaggerated, we still have a conflict where one side was *greatly* outnumbered by the other. There would have been almost 43 Persians per single Spartan.

Xerxes I of Persia had a formidable army, by all accounts, and was hell-bent on invading all of Greece and conquering it completely. King Leonidas in Sparta, naturally, had other ideas. The two faced off in Thermopylae, which, crucially, had a geography that heavily favored the Spartans. The area was essentially a narrow passage that meant Persia's advantage in number was greatly reduced. Both sides were armed and ready to fight. A messenger is said to have told a Spartan general, "Our arrows will block out the sun." The general, unfazed, simply replied, "Then we will fight in the shade."

For two long, hard days, Leonida's led his army to fend off the Persians, but the Persians must have realized at some point who they were up against. The Spartans took immense pride in their identities as warriors. Their military training was not just physically grueling and demanding, but they were mentally tough, too, knowing to their very bones that they would never, ever surrender or show even a splinter of weakness to the enemy. Basically, the Spartans would probably have been very flattered by their portrayal in Snyder's film!

They fought hard, with the Persians continually demanding surrender. The Spartans refused. Somehow, they maintained their energy and managed to take their toll on the Persians, killing thousands of their men. They took the credo of "do it or die trying" to the next level. At one point, there was a traitor by the name of Ephialtes, who told the Persians about a path that would allow them to advance on Leonidas and outflank his army. When he found out, Leonidas responded by creating a defensive rear-guard of around 1500 men – in these were the notable 300 Spartans, around 400 Thebans, 700 Thespians, and a few hundred slaves from other regions. If the accounts are to be believed, these men also fought bravely and relentlessly, never wavering in their strength and determination, even though, strategically, they had been placed there as a sacrifice that would buy the rest of the army some time to retreat and formulate a fresh plan against the Persians.

After three long and bloody days, the Spartans declared a decisive victory, and Xerxes retreated, his attack unsuccessful. Inspired by their miraculous victory, the Greeks went on to win further battles at Salamis and Plataea, effectively putting an end to the Persian's grand plans of invasion. The 300 who courageously gave their lives were ever after held as heroes, and their story still inspires today, not just in the 2006 movie but in countless documentaries and books, too. Today, you can see a memorial at Thermopylae that bears the words, "Stranger, go tell the Spartans, that here, obedient to their words we lie."

Some historians claim that the selfless sacrifice of these men actually had more of an influence over Greece's ultimate success than those who fought the Persians afterwards. Why? Because of what their profound act of bravery symbolized. Put yourself in the shoes of a Persian warrior who had to fight the Greeks after knowing that they were determined enough to lay down their lives strategically, if necessary, in order to serve their nation. Imagine encountering a man on the battlefield that you knew was *that* committed. The memory of what unfolded on those three days in Thermopylae cemented the reputation of the Spartans, which served to galvanize them in future battles in a way more effective than any literal armor or weaponry. It sent a powerful message: "We are fearless. We will stop at literally nothing."

Consider also the Greek soldiers who fought in the memory of those who fell for the cause. How insignificant would their own challenges and fears have seemed, when others had paid the ultimate price? Because of what the 300 did at Thermopylae, the Spartans had a name to live up to. They could all take part in the shared knowledge that they were warriors of a different order all together, and this must have given them immense courage and grit when it really mattered.

It's important to understand that, at the time, the Spartans would have understood their violence as a freedom fight against the threatened enslavement of the Persian empire. It's also important to understand the cultural context of the Spartans, which would have allowed them to consider the act of personal sacrifice far more easily than modern men could perhaps understand. A related story will illustrate. Before the battle, the Spartan's sages began to report bad omens and concluded that the gods were displeased with their decision to kill Persian ambassadors sent to Sparta by Xerxe's father Darius. To rectify the situation, two Spartans, called Sperthias and Bulis, volunteered to go to Persia and hand themselves over as sacrifices to atone.

On the way, the two men encountered a Persian general, who told them that Xerxes would likely receive them as honored guests, and that it was in their interests to find a way to cooperate with him. The Spartans were insulted. They did not want the "one world ruled by one master" that the Persians were trying to create. These two men had zero qualms about telling the general that they valued their freedom more than they did their very lives.

So, we can see that the Spartans were not merely aggressive blowhards who triumphed in battle – they were supremely principled and dignified men who flat out refused to set aside their own liberty. Each soldier understood that he was fighting for something much, much more important than his own life – he was fighting for the free spirit of Sparta itself. Frank Miller was an author who created a graphic novel about the battle of Thermopylae and describes Greece at the time as a "an island of reason and freedom in a sea of mysticism and tyranny." When the

Spartans were told to lay down their arms, they reportedly said, "Come and get them." Perhaps we can understand why the film was so loved by American audiences, especially second amendment fans!

Nobel Prize-winning author Sir William Golding said of the battle, "It is not just that the human spirit reacts directly and beyond all argument to story of sacrifice and courage...it is because, way back at the hundredth remove, that company stood in the right line of history. A little of Leonidas lies in the fact that I can go where I like and write what I like. He contributed to setting us free."

It is not just that the battle of Thermopylae was an impressive military victory that showed immense strength and courage. What won people's admiration was that it was a battle for freedom. Granted, the Spartans were not, as some would like to believe, champions of the free world in general, and they were known to be ruthless with their own slaves and do deals with the Persians that threatened the freedom of their own countrymen when it suited them.

Even though the historical context is a little more complicated, though, we can still appreciate, all these hundreds of years later, the sheer immenseness of the troops' conviction. At some point, they willingly and gladly lay down their lives for a cause they believed in more than life itself. What could be more impressive than conviction that strong?

When it comes to resilience and discipline, we can see too that the ability of the Spartans to fight when drastically outnumbered stemmed not just from their actions, but from their mindset. Because they were tapping into a powerful cause they believed in with all their heart, they found strength to fight brutally for three days. Because this cause was so much bigger than them, they were able to rise to the challenge and become, effectively, so much more than they were. Had they clung to their lives and retreated in terror and cowardice, they would have survived – but that's all. They would have won none of the glory and grandeur that we now associate so freely with the Spartans and their victory.

This principle was at the heart of Spartan society, and it played a massive role in their reputation as fearsome warriors. They lived their lives by three main virtues: discipline, obedience, and courage. Military training started young, and physical prowess was valued all throughout the culture, for men and women.

Another thing to consider is that the battle at Thermopylae was, hands-down, a complete loss for the Greeks. The brave 300 didn't ward off the hundreds of thousands of Persians. They all died. If the metric for success is number of men still standing, then the Spartans were utterly thrashed. But it is curious how often non-historians wrongly *assume* that this battle was one where "the 300 Spartans beat a million Persians." Why do they assume that the Spartans won? Because, in the long view, they did.

Today, most people simply believe that the Spartans were especially brave and badass, but their culture was extremely complex (and far from perfect). Sparta was a militarist state and trained its boys from birth to fight. Mothers would bathe their newborns in wine to test their strength, and take them before the Gerousia to see if they were fit to live, and boys would be trained to fight from 7 years old. If not, the baby was tossed into a chasm. If a Spartan died, a gravestone would be supplied only if the man died in victorious battle or the women in childbirth or divine service.

Boys lived communally, being fed "just the right amount for them never to become sluggish through being too full, while also giving them a taste of what it is not to have enough" and being punished if they were not quick or witty enough. A man was expected to be subordinate to his unit and always responsible to his comrades in arms.

Spartan women reportedly enjoyed more status and power than was typical in the rest of the world at the time, but there were cultural practices that many would balk at today. The Spartans were early proponents of a kind of eugenics and practiced a form of wife-sharing. Since they believed that only the physically fittest Spartans should breed, some older husbands sought younger men to impregnate their wives, or if a woman had been successful and prolific in childbirth, a man might request she bear his child. Considering how many Spartans would have routinely been killed in battle, this focus on producing as many able-bodied babies makes more sense!

There is even a term to describe admiration and obsession with ancient Spartan culture: *laconophilia*. During its own time, Sparta was a place of fascination and awe, even though prominent figures like Aristotle believed them misguided and short-sighted. Whether you consider the Spartans an inspirational model or not, it's hard not to be impressed by just what is possible when people are ruthlessly, 100% determined to fulfil their life's mission and purpose. When people are fired up this way, they become unstoppable. In our modern world, there are few who could claim a belief of that strength, and perhaps this is what we admire in the Spartans: their unwavering certainty.

Resilience doesn't come from nowhere. It is not something that we can conjure up by sheer willpower alone. Rather, it is a result of the mindset we hold and the core belief we allow to power us, as though it were an engine running at the center of our lives. Discipline is not some free-floating habit that we only have to claim. It is discipline *in the service of something*. If we home in on what that something is, then we are inspired and motivated to act towards it, no matter what.

Truth be told, few modern people can imagine genuinely pledging their lives to their commanders or the military integrity of their nation, but to the extent that they lack commitment and devotion to *any* cause, they will also lack discipline, courage, purpose, focus, and resilience.

The Spartans were not some special superhuman breed. They were just human beings. However, they were human beings who believed in something. In committing themselves to a cause greater than their own lives, they achieved greatness and legacy, and they were able to endure everything -even death – on the path to that legacy.

If you are facing a difficult time, you may be tempted to give up, to start to feel like a victim, to look around for others to blame for your problems, or to hope quietly that someone will save you. Here, you are faced with a profound choice: you can abandon your path, give up your goal, and perhaps continue on with a host of excuses for why you never achieved what you set out to do. This may feel good in the short-term, but in the longer term, it will undermine your sense of confidence and self-belief. You might convince others, for example, that something was "impossible" or not your fault, but you will know deep down whether you could have done more, and that can quietly eat away at your sense of integrity.

The other path you can take is more difficult. You'll *actively* have to take the path– it can't be taken for you. However, in many ways, this is the easier route. If you dwell on what is impossible, difficult, unpleasant or unfair, you are powerless. But if you act – even if that action is unsuccessful – you are no longer powerless. Even though the Spartans were slaughtered at Thermopylae, this was something they understood. This was what allowed them to blaze on in glory, even as they handed over their lives.

Everyday example

In 1967, protester George Harris delicately placed a carnation flower into the barrel of an M14 rifle pointed at him and the rest of the crowd marching on the pentagon to protest the Vietnam war. George was just 18 at the time, and though his gesture certainly didn't end the war or change things for the people who lost their lives fighting it, it did have some effect. A photographer captured the moment, and this simple gesture would ultimately have a powerful influence on the antiwar movement in the sixties and become a defining symbol of the zeitgeist. The iconic act, though seemingly small and insignificant at the time, inspired countless others for years afterwards, just as the implications of the battle at Thermopylae would ripple out into all of history.

The Spartans' lessons:

- The Spartans lived by a set of principles and core beliefs that guided everything they did, and this is ultimately what allowed them to act with strength, conviction, and discipline. When you commit to a cause and belief greater than yourself, you become unstoppable, and even death itself is no longer something you fear.
- We don't have to believe the Spartans were perfect in every way to appreciate the courage it took to live life the way they lived it. We can be inspired in our own lives and ask, *what do we care about so deeply that we would be happy to die for it?* Knowing the answer to that question allows you to access vast stores of grit, courage, and strength.
- Be active. Be tough. For the Spartans, physical prowess was everything, but we can follow suit by making strength – all

kinds of strength – a non-negotiable part of our personal identity. If life seems scary and challenging, then train yourself to be equal to the challenge. Work hard, dedicate yourself, and choose toughness even when it would be easier to fold.

Chapter 11: Spartacus and the servile wars

From the famed bravery and sacrifice of the Spartans, we now move on to the story of one warrior in particular, who also won the hearts and minds of people for generations after he lived: Spartacus. Here too we find themes of freedom triumphing over slavery, of heroic bravery, and of finding glorious victory in the face of considerable adversity. To cut a long and fascinating story short, Spartacus escaped slavery along with about 70 other gladiators. He then went on to raise an army of about 100,000 and defeat the greatest military establishment ever known – a full 6 times over 4 years. His efforts have easily made him one of history's favorite underdogs and the man who did the most when he had nothing to lose.

Let's start at the beginning of his story. Spartacus was born in Thrace, which in the ancient world was an area including the countries of Turkey, Bulgaria, and Greece today. The ancient world was one few of us can imagine, and slavery, poverty, and war were a part of life. There are theories that Spartacus first served in the Roman army, but, perhaps because he rebelled against them, he was sold off into slavery and then sent in 73 B.B to "gladiator school" (ludus) in Capua.

Here, he was a kind of heavyweight gladiator called a *murmillo* and was made to carry a scutum (a large shield) and a gladius (a broad, straight sword around 18 inches in length). Ancient Rome was a bloodthirsty and brutal civilization, where slaves were forced to fight to the death for the amusement of the elites and the public in general. Sometimes, unwilling gladiators were pitted against wild animals, violent criminals, or even each other. Gladiators were seen as disposable and worthless; some were indeed famous and rich, but none were free, and all could be sentenced to death at the whim of the emperor.

Spartacus, along with dozens of other slaves and captives in the ludus, plotted to escape to freedom. Using stolen kitchen utensils, they seized wagons, armor, and weapons and used them to defeat the troops sent after them. They went on to plunder the area around Capua, and as they went, their message of hope, bravery, and insurrection inspired other slaves, who joined them. Followers soon gathered the cause, likely taken in by Spartacus' inspiring tale and wanting to mete out justice and retaliation on the Romans who had enslaved them.

In total, Spartacus' original 70 or so gladiators had gathered around 100,000 men, using innovative guerrilla tactics to keep the pursuing Romans at bay, and eventually gathering on the iconic Mount Vesuvius. A year in, they had organized themselves to march to Gaul (France today) to stage a revolution, and their efforts would be called the Servile War, or the Gladiator's War. At first, this rag-tag bunch of rebels was not taken very seriously, but with each victory, the growing army began to worry Rome.

In 72 B.C, in Gaul, they continue to fight against the Romans but then changed course and headed south again, likely to advance on Sicily. By this time, General Marcus Licinius Crassus realized he needed to assemble an army to neutralize the threat. Another army led by the Roman general Pompey also worked hard to suppress the rebellion. In 71 B.C., however, Spartacus' army was defeated at Lucania, and Spartacus was said to have died during the battle, while 6000 of the men were captured by the Romans and crucified.

Like the people of Sparta and the battle of Thermopylae, the servile wars also continued to inspire subsequent revolutions and uprisings all over the world. For example, the Spartacist League was a social group in 1916 Germany that took inspiration from the ex-gladiator in their attempt to overthrow the German government. There are countless other examples of rebel groups, bandits, and even sports teams taking Spartacus' name in a bid to take part symbolically in some of the bravery he showed in resisting his subjugators.

Not much is known about Spartacus' early life, but by many accounts, as an adult, he was a strong, capable, and principled leader that coordinated a hoard of vastly different individuals towards one common cause – their freedom. Though it's true that historians now understand that Spartacus was not actually attempting social revolution or the complete abolition of slavery in the Republic, he was nevertheless an inspiring figure that proved to generations afterwards that even a man who has nothing can be a powerful force to be reckoned with.

In fact, there had already been *two* unsuccessful servile wars (Rome had a bit of slave problem), and the third one led by Spartacus was really a complex series of many separate battles and skirmishes, most of which have not been comprehensively documented. It would take many more years for the brutality of the gladiator era finally to come to end – the last game was held in January in 404 AD, hundreds of years after Spartacus' time. The practice finally fell out of favor, not primarily because of its brutality, but rather because Christian critics at the time objected to the use of pagan ritual during the games.

Plutarch claimed that Spartacus killed his own horse in front of his army, saying, "If we win, I will have no need of this horse because we will have thousands of Roman horses, and if we lose, I will have no use of a horse." Though we don't know much about Spartacus as a man, we can glean a lot from this quote and the determination it showed. For decades after his death (and his body was not found), Spartacus was forgotten, and there were no written records from Spartacus or his army. Considering that "history is written by the victors" and that many of his troops would have been illiterate and uneducated slaves, this is not surprising.

It was only in France in the 1760s that new interest in this period of history surfaced, at a time when political freedom was again a rousing flavor of the day. The story of Spartacus was eagerly seized by Europe, and Karl Marx cited him as a hero and ultimate symbol of class struggle. If it weren't for the few documented lines of evidence that historians examined, the tale of Spartacus might have been doomed to obscurity and forgotten. But something about him and his struggle lived on. In fact, one of the only things that remains after thousands of years is the fact that Spartacus must have been an exemplary, principled man who fought hard for freedom and justice.

Even without the details, we can learn a lot from Spartacus. Picture a group of miscellaneous slaves, convicts, and captives, all from different regions and with different languages and intentions. Somehow, Spartacus managed to speak to and inspire tens of thousands of such people into one powerful, cohesive group. This was a man who had very little military training, but he knew how to speak to the hearts of the men he'd eventually win over. He was generous with the spoils of their battles and divided the bounty equally amongst the men, no matter who they were. This sense of fair play likely won the loyalty of men who might have been enslaved and abused all their lives.

We can also infer a few more things about Spartacus' strategy overall. After one battle, where the gathered slave army defeated Romans led by both Gellius and Lentulus, Spartacus captured 400 Roman soldiers and forced them to fight one another – just like gladiators. Why? We can imagine that Spartacus did this for two reasons: he wanted to give his men a visceral feeling of their victory, knowing that the sight of this justice (or, to be frank, plain old revenge) would give them enormous confidence and motivation to continue. There's a darker side to this, too: Spartacus is also said to have crucified a Roman soldier one day, so that his troops could see what would await them should the Romans capture him.

Spartacus also knew that the story of the fate of these Roman soldiers would travel the grapevine and reach the ears of those in power in Rome.

It's likely that Spartacus knew that the uprising could not continue on forever, and that he would at some point lose his life. Even understanding the risk and the eventual outcome, he did what he could to motivate and encourage his troops. This kind of vision teaches us that our resilience is not just for ourselves – when we are disciplined, strong, and determined, we can inspire others. We are worthy of leading others.

Spartacus knew that his men had been trained to use a sword, but instead of fighting as gladiators for the amusement of cruel Romans, they would reclaim these skills and use them for their own liberation. Spartacus also knew that there were incredible depths of hatred bubbling in the hearts of the freed slaves – and he would do his best to channel that energy into something noble. His men must have recognized what we still see in Spartacus today: he was, for the downtrodden, a symbol of spirited resistance against oppression and a victor in the eternal fight between just and unjust.

We don't have to have lived through such adversity or orchestrated a slave uprising to practice some of Spartacus' principled courage in our own lives. Spartacus teaches us that, if we are mistreated or subjugated, we don't have to take it lying down! And sometimes, starting from absolute zero is an advantageous position to be in. There is a brilliant irony here – in the gladiatorial ring, the Romans had taught Spartacus to fight for his life. So he did! But this time, on his own terms.

Spartacus is believed to have said, "I am no martyr upon a cross, yet I will gladly risk life so those deserving can live." For him, as it was for the Spartans, he saw only two options: freedom or death. He would not submit. If your cause is greater than your own life, then you are never too weak or too subjugated to fight. Dignity, virtue, and honor are there in abundance for those who would anchor themselves in what they know to be right and just. We can imagine that not only did Spartacus understand this, but he was able to communicate his passion to those who fought alongside him.

Few of us in the developed Western world have to face injustices of the scale that Spartacus and his men did. But perhaps his story can give us courage to live a little larger anyway, to take risks, and to speak up against injustice when we see it. If you are facing adversity in life, or if you feel like you've been dealt an unfair hand, take heart and remind yourself that you always have the power to decide how you will respond.

Spartacus had *nothing*. He was stripped of any military honors, sold like a piece of meat, and forced to do the Roman's bidding under threat of death. He would have owned very little, had no contact with his family, and even if he befriended a fellow gladiator, he might be forced to kill him at the whim of his captors. Yet still he did not lose courage. In fact, we can imagine that his sense of rage and indignation became a powerful source of energy that, channeled and focused, allowed him to pull off the military feats that made even Rome look up and pay attention.

If you are feeling beaten down by people who are stronger, richer, more powerful, or simply crueler than you, make a promise to yourself that you will not allow them to conquer your spirit, too. Seek out others in your predicament and find strength and purpose with them. Don't rage quietly about something you know isn't right – get up and do something about it. Use what you can. Remember that Spartacus began his epic journey with the theft of kitchen implements! If you need to start small, then do that. But *do something* – therein lies your salvation and sense of strength and resilience.

Sometimes, when we hear the word "resilience," it can conjure up feelings of having to *endure* awful things. We might look at a gladiator in the ring and call him resilient because he effectively bears his own servitude and works hard not to let his own suffering break him. His strength in this context is certainly noble, but Spartacus shows us that there is also resilience in our *refusal* to tolerate what we cannot accept.

Is there something in your life that you're quietly enduring because you think that resisting it would be hopeless? Only you can say whether your continued tolerance is a sign of wise forbearance or simply evidence of being cowardly. Many of us will read the story of Spartacus and think, "Well that's fine for *him*, but I'm not like that. I could never do anything remotely like that."

But in a way, isn't this deliberate "playing small" a form of enslavement? If we are trapped in our own limiting beliefs and convinced that we can never genuinely change our lot in life, aren't we even more enslaved than the captives in Spartacus' army? These are big questions and require big answers from us. But Spartacus was a man who saw the size of the challenge and didn't balk. Taking on the Roman republic was a staggering feat – few would even have the courage to dare.

But Spartacus did. And he did so with far fewer resources than many of us take for granted today.

In your own life, consider where you may have taken the coward's road and tolerated injustice or servitude where you knew it was wrong. Have there been times when you were silent when you should have spoken up? What would be possible if you connected passionately with others and made a stand against something you cared about, rather than shrugging your shoulders and saying, "Well, that's just the way it is"?

If you can begin to answer these questions for yourself, and act on them, then you will begin to understand what leadership is and exactly what was at stake all those thousands of years ago when the man named Spartacus decided to take matters into his own hands.

Everyday example

Few battles are as ambitious as Spartacus'. Most are small, but they still matter. Jade is working a new job that is extremely high pressured. She gradually becomes aware, however, of certain ways that the company does business that leave her feeling uneasy. One day, she learns of a colleague being dismissed for raising a sexual harassment complaint against a superior. Though the staff seems content to brush it all under the rug, Jade's conscience won't let her rest.

One day, she speaks up about her concerns, fully accepting that, as a newcomer, her job is in danger. To her surprise, she learns many others feel the same way and thus begins a slow but steady process of change in her company work culture that she never could have imagined. In time, she becomes respected and valued for her integrity.

Spartacus' lessons:

- Spartacus was able to do what he did because he was exquisitely focused on his goal – justice. Freedom is being outside of the control and dominion of any other being except yourself. Even if you are enslaved, you can emancipate yourself first by refusing to submit to injustice.
- It may feel like you have nothing but use what you do have, reach out to others, and do whatever it takes to get where you want to be.
- Finally, there is no virtue in tolerating something you cannot bear, instead of summoning up the courage to fight against it. Whether you succeed or not is beside the point – you assert your own autonomy and dignity in merely taking a stand.

Summary Guide

CHAPTER 1: ERNEST SHACKLETON AND HIS CREW: AN INSPIRING STORY OF STRENGTH AND SURVIVAL

- Find purpose. Seek a deeper meaning and significance in your life, and, if it strengthens you, anchor yourself in religion or spirituality. Shackleton never felt alone during his most arduous challenges, and that's because he was a man of faith.
- When times are challenging, keep sane and even-keeled by engrossing yourself in the details of day to day life. Keep a routine, look after the basics of life, and if need be, find relieving distractions when things get especially difficult.
- Finally, don't give up. When you encounter a challenge, reframe the way you look at it: it's not the end. Difficulties are not a sign that your journey is over, just that the route has changed. Difficulties are just things to overcome. If you have hope, then you'll be prepared and ready to grasp opportunity when it does finally come your way.

CHAPTER 2: BEETHOVEN: NOT EVEN DEAFNESS WAS AN EXCUSE

- Dig deep and connect to your overarching life's purpose. What matters most to you? What do you care about achieving here on earth more than anything else? Allow this conviction to give you strength to weather any obstacles on the way.
- Be true to yourself. Beethoven really did things his way. This wasn't always easy, but his commitment to his own authentic artistic vision gave him the courage to try things that others might not have wanted to risk. In difficult times, lean on your strengths – those unique insights and perspectives that nobody else could offer the world but you.
- Finally, be adaptable. When one path closes to you, look around for the paths that are still open. Refuse to dwell on what is missing, what is not working, or what is difficult. Instead, constantly turn your attention to what is possible, what resources you still have, and what opportunities are still there to be tapped.

CHAPTER 3: THOMAS CARLYLE AND WRITING *THE FRENCH REVOLUTION*

- Live large. Take your mission seriously and choose to be a hero in your own epic saga of triumph and overcoming.
- Endless resilience is possible when you tap into your deepest convictions and beliefs. Find that thing you are most passionate and resolute about and allow it to animate all your efforts. That way, any obstacle is perceived as a minor inconvenience, just a trifle on the bigger, more important path you're on.
- Read. Educate yourself and absorb knowledge wherever you can. Carlyle built a complex and sophisticated worldview because he was able to read widely, and this view would forever act as a buffer against adversity and a source of strength during dark times.

CHAPTER 4: THOMAS EDISON, THE LIGHTBULB, AND THE POWER OF TRYING 1000 TIMES

- Change the way you think about failure. Challenge and adversity are the best teachers you will ever have in life. Instead of getting upset when things don't go your way, become curious about what happened and why, then try again, but this time do it better!
- Forget about things like genius or innate talent. They're nice to have, but the people who get ahead are simply those who are willing to work hard and do it consistently.
- Adopt a growth mindset and constantly turn your attention, not to what is going wrong, but to the infinite world of the possible. There **is** a way out of your current predicament – how are you going to get from here to there?

CHAPTER 5: COLONEL SANDERS – A DELICIOUS STORY OF REJECTION

- It's never too late to start over, no matter how old you are. Colonel Sanders started over in his sixties and still managed to create a business empire that would

overtake those he might have considered younger and more talented than him. The past doesn't define who you are now, and it doesn't define who you can be in the future.
- Success takes time, and it takes consistent, diligent effort – there are no shortcuts for anyone. You don't have to be superhuman to be resilient and disciplined. All you need to do is refuse to give up. Don't pay attention to the flashy success stories you read about in the media – true accomplishment doesn't happen overnight, so be patient.
- If you're facing a setback, loss, or disappointment, consider adjusting your expectations. Sometimes being mentally strong and tough is simply a matter of not expecting the important things in life to be easy the first time around!

CHAPTER 6: GALILEO AND THE BRAVERY TO STAND ALONE

- Be true to yourself. Have faith in your own judgment and stick to your firmly held convictions, even if you have to do so alone. This will imbue you with

enormous courage and resilience in the face of challenges, because you will believe in yourself.
- Be humble. Use your intellect and your reason to the best of your ability, but always be willing to learn more. Don't boast about your conclusions but allow them to guide your convictions quietly from within. If you're lost, stay curious and return to the faculties that you're blessed with – keep asking questions and be brave enough to discover the answers.
- Realize that, sadly, you will not always be rewarded for your diligence and persistence. Instead, seek to find meaning and purpose in your work, whatever it is, so that it inspires you even if nobody else recognizes its value. Then, you will have tapped a well of strength that very few will be able to match!

CHAPTER 7: THE BATTLE OF ZAMA: THE ROMAN'S SECRET TO WINNING

- Don't give up. Failure, loss, and disappointment are not the end of the line. Learn, try again, and do better the next time around. Have the courage to

accept what can be improved and, instead of dwelling on the pain of your defeat, get proactive and start *doing*.
- It's cowardly to blame others for your shortcomings or to get angry at life in general for not being fair. If you've been justly beaten, accept it graciously. Don't be a bad loser. In fact, if you can, try to welcome even painful challenges in life as an opportunity to learn and be better. Like the Romans, we can all build monuments to those who have taught us our most difficult lessons.
- Hard work is a wonderful remedy for pain and loss. Resilience is not just about passively accepting your lot – you can empower yourself by taking action, and this will make any hardship 100 times easier to bear.

CHAPTER 8: ALEXANDER THE GREAT AND THE LAND BRIDGE TO TYRE ISLAND

- When facing an obstacle, don't get despondent or give up – simply become curious about **how** you will get around it

(take the fact that you will get around it as a foregone conclusion!)
- Believe in yourself. No need to be a megalomaniac of Alexander the Great proportions, but don't allow others to tell you what you are and are not capable of doing. This, rather than self-pity and feeling victimized, can bless you with far more dignity and resilience.
- If your plans aren't working, change the plans. If the story takes a bad turn, change the story. If you're losing the game, change the rules of the game until you are winning! The most successful people in history didn't wait to be given permission to believe in their own competence – they just barged ahead and believed it anyway.

CHAPTER 9: JULIUS CAESAR AND THE BATTLE OF ALESIA

- No matter how bleak things look, stay calm and take heart: you always have the power to choose your response, and you can often turn a disadvantage into an advantage simply by changing your perspective.

- When faced with a challenge or obstacle, try to think outside of the box and imagine a solution beyond your current way of thinking. Understand the rules, like Caesar, and then be brave and audacious enough to rewrite them completely to your advantage.
- There is never any reason for despair or giving up – things can and often do change at a moment's notice. Stay alert and take whatever action you can, reminding yourself that, if there are no opportunities on the table that you like, you can create opportunities. The double rampart idea didn't exist before the battle of Alesia – what novel solution to your own current problems is just one ingenious idea away?

CHAPTER 10: THE BATTLE OF THERMOPYLAE

- The Spartans lived by a set of principles and core beliefs that guided everything they did, and this is ultimately what allowed them to act with strength, conviction, and discipline. When you commit to a cause and belief greater than

yourself, you become unstoppable, and even death itself is no longer something you fear.
- We don't have to believe the Spartans were perfect in every way to appreciate the courage it took to live life the way they lived it. We can be inspired in our own lives and ask, *what do we care about so deeply that we would be happy to die for it?* Knowing the answer to that question allows you to access vast stores of grit, courage, and strength.
- Be active. Be tough. For the Spartans, physical prowess was everything, but we can follow suit by making strength – all kinds of strength – a non-negotiable part of our personal identity. If life seems scary and challenging, then train yourself to be equal to the challenge. Work hard, dedicate yourself, and choose toughness even when it would be easier to fold.

CHAPTER 11: SPARTACUS AND THE SERVILE WARS

- Spartacus was able to do what he did because he was exquisitely focused on his goal – justice. Freedom is being

outside of the control and dominion of any other being except yourself. Even if you are enslaved, you can emancipate yourself first by refusing to submit to injustice.
- It may feel like you have nothing but use what you do have, reach out to others, and do whatever it takes to get where you want to be.
- Finally, there is no virtue in tolerating something you cannot bear, instead of summoning up the courage to fight against it. Whether you succeed or not is beside the point – you assert your own autonomy and dignity in merely taking a stand.

www.ingramcontent.com/pod-product-compliance
Lightning Source LLC
Chambersburg PA
CBHW020534080526
44583CB00013B/863